Woven Fine

ABOUT THE AUTHOR

Susan Hardwick is an Anglican priest in Coventry Diocese. She trained for the ordained ministry at Queen's College, Birmingham (1982-5), since when she has worked for the Coventry Diocese in various areas of ministry. Susan Hardwick was priested in 1994 at Coventry Cathedral.

She is married to an Anglican priest and has two grown-up children.

Susan Hardwick is the author of *A Weaving of Peace* (Kevin Mayhew, 1996).

Woven Fine

A Spiritual Tapestry of Sorrow & Joy

SUSAN HARDWICK

Kevin Mayhew

First published in 1997 by
KEVIN MAYHEW LTD
Rattlesden
Bury St Edmunds
Suffolk IP30 0SZ

© 1997 Kevin Mayhew Ltd

0 1 2 3 4 5 6 7 8 9

The right of Susan Hardwick to be identified as the author
of this work has been asserted by her in accordance with the
Copyright, Designs and Patents Act 1988.

All rights reserved. No part of this publication may be
reproduced, stored in a retrieval system, or transmitted,
in any form or by any means, electronic, mechanical,
photocopying, recording or otherwise,
without the prior written permission
of the publisher.

ISBN 0 86209 940 4
Catalogue No 1500087

Cover illustration: Dandelions, by Simon Palmer (living artist)
Private Collection/Bridgeman Art Library, London

Edited by Peter Dainty
Typesetting by Louise Hill
Printed and bound in Great Britain

FOREWORD

Life, for all of us, is a closely woven tapestry of good times and of bad, of heartaches and of laughter, of sorrows and of joys.

From the heights of ecstasy to the depths of despair it is our human gifting to be able to experience a whole range of emotions. The more we open ourselves to life, and to living it fully, the more keenly we experience the highs and the lows that are an inescapable part of the life we have been given.

Woven Fine is for all those who seek to understand and to explore the sorrows and the joys of their own lives, as well as for those who wish to walk more closely with others through their experiences.

In this book reflections, meditations, prayers, poetry, stories, personal experiences, quotations from the Bible and from literature, are woven together into a tapestry of many textures and colours.

Like its sister book *A Weaving of Peace*, published in July 1996, *Woven Fine* is a radical spirituality and is written for all travellers, for sceptics, for those who struggle to find an authentic and stable faith – a faith that is real – in an ever-changing world.

Every book it is said is, in part, an autobiography. By this I suppose is meant that, if it is to ring true with those who read it, it must contain a great deal of the author. However, no person lives and grows in isolation, and the multicoloured threads of the lives and thinking of those who have touched my life and influenced me, in all sorts of ways, are bound to be woven into the person I am. And the same, I suppose, must be true in reverse. Thus, in a very real sense, I am in the world and the world is in me. For all the threads which have enriched my life, I give thanks to God.

SUSAN HARDWICK

DEDICATION

This book is dedicated
to the memory of
my parents
and my grandparents,
in especial gratitude for the rich tapestry
of their lives,
so many threads of which
have woven down the years
to become an intimate part
of my life.

Joy and Woe

are woven fine,

A Clothing for

the Soul divine;

Underneath each

grief and pine

Runs a joy

with silken twine . . .

WILLIAM BLAKE
from *Auguries of Innocence*

ACKNOWLEDGEMENTS

The publishers wish to express their gratitude to the following for permission to include copyright material in this book:

The GMB General Union for extract from 50 'reasons' given by employers for cutting jobs.

Gujarat Sahitya Prakash, Anand, Gujarat, 388 001 India, for extracts from *The Song of the Bird, One Minute Wisdom* and *Sadhana: A Way to God* by Anthony de Mello SJ.

HarperCollins Publishers, 77-85 Fulham Palace Road, London W6 8JB, for the extract from *Mister God this is Anna* (Fynn), William Collins Sons & Co, 1974.

Vintage Books, a division of Random House Inc., 201 East 50th Street, New York, New York 10022, USA, for the extract from *The Doctor and the Soul* (Victor Frankl), Vintage Books, 1986.

Bill Wallace, New Zealand for his quotation 'In the letting go . . .' (18)

Scripture quotations are taken from the *New Jerusalem Bible*, published by Darton Longman & Todd.

Every effort has been made to trace the owners of copyright material and we hope that no copyright has been infringed. Pardon is sought and apology is made if the contrary be the case and a correction will be made in any reprint of this book.

CONTENTS

Textures	11
EMPTINESS AND SPACE	
Unable to Pray	14
Silence	19
Lonely	24
Space	29
Despairing	34
Wonder	39
LOSS AND GAIN	
Too Young to Die	46
Letting Go	51
Loss	56
New Experiences	62
Unemployed	67
Work	72
CAUGHT AND HELD	
Addicted	79
Talents	83
Bad Memories	88
Communication	94
Stress	99
Words . . . Art . . . Music	104
SHADOW AND LIGHT	
Suffering	111
Laughter	117
Injustice	121
Beauty	127
Frightened	131
Thankfulness	136
REFERENCES	143

TEXTURES

A Parable of the paradox of the Joyful Sorrow and the Sorrowful Joy

Imagine:
a simple loom
with just the
horizontal threads.
These are the years
along which
the soul travels.

Watch:
as the shuttle weaves
in and out,
out and in,
thread on thread,
layer on layer,
rainbow patterns
of every texture
and of every shade,
complex and
multi-coloured,
echoes seen before
and repeated
in different context
or hue.

Look closely now:
and see where light
gives way to
streaks of grey
and how dark
is shot through
with the Son.

EMPTINESS AND SPACE

Unable to Pray

> Never worry about anything;
> but tell God all your desires
> of every kind,
> in prayer and petition
> shot through with gratitude.
> (Philippians 4:6)

Wonderful words – but what if you are unable to pray? What if you feel that, where formerly there was a sense of communication, now there is only emptiness and desert?

'Throwing gravel at some far-off seemingly uninhabited window in heaven' is how the poet R. S. Thomas graphically described it.

During an extended stay in the Holy Land I visited the desert a number of times.

Small wonder that the writers of both the Old and New Testaments so often used it as an analogy for aspects of the spiritual life.

Dry, arid, often rocky and bleak, scorching hot by day and shiveringly cold by night, with a silence so deep that it seems to shout back at you – and sand that creeps insidiously into your shoes, clothes, hair, mouth, nostrils, eyes and ears.

It is easy to imagine that you are the only person left alive in the world.

The two essentials of that land, water and shade, are conspicuous by their general absence.

I imagined Jesus during his forty days and forty nights in the desert, seated on a rock or walking the sand, eyes cast down in deep thought, or cast up in deep prayer.

Was God, I wondered, always present as solace and comfort for him in this lonely place? Or did Jesus know times of desolation, and of the apparent absence of God? Were there times when the outer aridity and dryness reflected that of his own soul – and was he then unable to pray?

If Jesus did indeed know personally all our temptations and difficulties then, presumably, this most common of spiritual experiences must at times also have been his.

Was he caught up to highest heaven, and cast down to lowest earth, in his moods and feelings? Was it part of God's mighty plan, even for him? Did even Jesus need to be gently shaped and moulded for his mightiest of tasks?

Jesus was so attuned to the Father's will. He could so easily have felt there was nothing more for him to learn. And yet he trusted the Father's judgement on this, as in all things, and allowed himself to be led out into the wilderness far from the solace and comfort of others. Far from the flattering curiosity of the disciples sent along by John the Baptist.

There in the desert he submitted meekly – and that does not mean pathetically but obediently, trustingly – to being opened wide open, and turned inside out, by this gruelling experience.

Perhaps, then, we should not be surprised when the Father wishes to do the same to us. Very often, the sense of being unable to pray is part of this opening and deepening process.

'Deep is calling to deep'

is the Psalmist's powerful description in Psalm 42:7.

God calls us out into the desert experience where we feel the aridness and the dryness of such a place, in order that he may deepen his relationship with us, and we with him. For God is never absent, although it may at times seem that way. He is sometimes screened from our view, but he is always there; watching over us, loving us; tenderly beckoning us closer to him.

It is very easy to mistake the cosy comfortable closeness of habit, found in many of our most intimate relationships, for love. But then, when we experience the real thing, we realise how much of a shadow was the former.

And so it is with prayer. We can mistake the cosy comfortable habit as the most perfect thing. But then God calls us, and moves us on, to something better and richer; and it is only then, looking back, that we can see how little the former reflected this new and deeper and more authentic relationship.

The literal translation, so I have read, of 'Pray constantly' (1 Thessalonians 5:17) is 'Come to rest'. Prayer is not something we do to God, so much as something he does in us.

So, when we feel we are unable to pray, it is sufficient to 'come to rest' in the Lord, just to be with him, in loving communing silence; allowing him to love us and to nurture us at the very deepest level of our being, far deeper than we can be aware.

> But look, I am going to lead her
> into the desert
> and speak to her heart.
> There I shall make the Vale of Achor*
> a gateway of hope.
> (Hosea 2:16, 17a)

It is sufficient that we trust that, in this desert time, God is working his will in us, and that all we have to do is to open ourselves up to this re-creating and reshaping; to know that God wills only our good, what is best for us, for we are each most precious to him.

> 'Not my will, but yours',

Jesus prayed in the Garden of Gesthemane; another desert place for him, although he was surrounded by olive trees and exotic plants.

So we need rather, perhaps, to be thankful for the desert times. For they are a sign, not of God's absence, but of God's

---

* The name means *valley of misfortune*

activity in us. What we must *not* do is to stop setting aside times just to be with God and to rest in his presence – unseen, unfelt maybe, but he is always closer to us than we are to ourselves.

> 'I shall instruct you and teach you the way to go;
> I shall not take my eyes off you',
> promises God in Psalm 32:8.

One evening, I watched the sun setting over the desert. As it slipped down behind the horizon everything blazed with a celestial artist's palette of colours, splashed with riotous abandonment across sky and sand alike. The dry grains of the latter were turned to liquid gold, and the former seemed to shout a paeon of praise to God the Creator. The shades and colours were so brilliant that my eyes ached.

And I knew, as surely as I have ever known anything, that there is indeed a God, and that such a God of glory and tender beauty could not will anything but the best for me, and for all his children.

> Teach me to pray,
> Lord,
> with the prayer of the trusting disciple
> who rests peacefully in the darkness
> of their inner self.
> Deep down,
> in the centre of their being,
> where you are to be found.

Teach me not to pray,
Lord,
when it is your desire
that I merely am,
resting as a child
in their
Father's arms.

Desert or town,
Lord,
mountain or plain,
you are there
before me,
beckoning me.

Deep

is

calling

to

deep

Amen.

True love and prayer become one
when prayer becomes impossible and
the heart has turned to stone. (1)

Silence

> Elected Silence, sing to me
> And beat upon my whorlèd ear,
> Pipe me to pastures still and be
> The music that I care to hear. (2)

Although I am a gregarious person and love to be with others, for as long as I can remember I have also needed space and silence in each day: time just to be on my own.

When I was a child, growing up in a large, busy and noisy house which always seemed to be filled with people of various ages, sizes and nationalities, I would disappear when I needed silence to various hiding-places – up a tree, in a den, or in the attic, or elsewhere: secret corners which, I fondly believed, were known only to me.

As an adult, it was easy when there were only other adults to consider. Your 'own time' was something you had the freedom to negotiate on an equal footing.

However, when my children came on the scene and family life began once more to resemble a Posy Simmonds cartoon, I had to readjust my horizons.

It is not so easy to 'negotiate' with babies and toddlers, as they do not seem quite to understand the word in the same way as an adult. Trying to tell them that you need some space and silence in each day in order for you to feel a whole person is like telling them that spinach is good for them when you know very well they detest it.

Please don't get me wrong, I loved every minute (well, practically) of being the mother of small children: the pride and joy in them and in their development; sharing intimately their joys and triumphs, their sorrows and their pain, and the privilege of knowing that I would be the first person whom they would want and need in any situation; the wondrous pleasures and anxieties and anguishes of parenthood – but I did still need that space and silence.

It was when my baby son decided he no longer needed to sleep during the day at precisely the same time as my toddler daughter started at playschool, and which effectively scotched that anticipated solution, I decided that perhaps the necessity to perceive things differently lay with me; that, if I was to achieve my precious goal and ambition, I was the one who would have to change, rather than expecting the rest of the world to adapt to me.

When I began to think about it in this new light, I made a discovery: perhaps I had been confusing outer, external silence with silence within.

I began to understand that if there was not silence within me, however much I created it in my external environment, there would still be a yearning left deep inside myself.

Perhaps then, I wondered, had I been seeking the wrong thing? In our noisy, sound-filled world there is not always silence to be had, and so was my peace of mind to rely upon finding this elusive external thing?

Or should I seek elsewhere? Should I, perhaps, be turning right round in my tracks in order to begin walking inward? It was worth a try.

That decision was the beginning of a great and exciting journey. And the strange thing was, it did not at all detract from the outer activity but, rather, enhanced it. Mysteriously, the more I practised this inner journeying, this inner seeking of silence, the more energy I seemed to have for the constant bustle and demand of my hectic life.

One day, two or three years later, I was encouraged to know that I really had made some progress with my self-imposed task, and that it had become noticeable even to others.

We had invited another family, with children the same age as our own, to tea.

It was raining, and so the children had decided to have a 'jam' (as in music) session in the dining room. One was on the piano, another on a recorder – which he had no idea how to play – a third was banging a metal spoon on various-sized saucepans, enthusiastically but with little sense of rhythm, and the fourth was banging the lids of the aforementioned saucepans together, again with much enthusiasm but with rather better timing than her brother. The fifth was on a very shrill tin whistle.

I was in the kitchen, next to the dining room, preparing the tea and rather enjoying the result of their efforts when the father of the other family came in. He shouted over their music, asking me how I could stand being in such close proximity to such dreadful bedlam without going *absolutely* mad.

At this point, my husband entered and said, 'Somehow, at times like these, she always seems to manage to withdraw to the centre of herself.'

'Huh!' muttered our friend. 'Some people have all the luck, don't they.'

'The disciple asked for a word of wisdom.
Said the Master, "Go, sit within your cell and your cell will teach you wisdom."
"But I have no cell. I am no monk."
"Of course you have a cell. Look within."' (3)

As the children got older and their needs changed, so I was more and more able to build in regular times of quiet. But it was not always easy, and often I had to decide what was really important to me, where my priorities lay, and then rearrange things accordingly.

Sometimes in the silence I feel as if I am returning to my original, my first, home – not to the home of my childhood, but prior to then; as if my little silence is linking into a far greater Silence that was there before the beginning of time;

before this wonderful world with its ceaseless activity was created.

'. . . how the silence surged softly backward . . .'

as Walter de la Mare perfectly put it in his poem, 'The Listener'. (4)

The deeper the silence the more I feel it sinking through, linking to, the deepest part of me to the point where, we are assured, God dwells in each one of us – dwelling in the silence which is beyond words.

There is a paradox here; the God of the storm so often also comes to us and blesses us from within the infinite depths of his silence.

In one of the most beloved of all Christmas carols, within the hushed stillness of that most silent and holy of nights, is described the example above all examples of God's silent gifting: the silent march of the stars across the sky, and the silent and loving vigil of the angels above the sleeping mortals:

> How silently, how silently,
> The wondrous gift is given!
> So God imparts to human hearts
> The blessings of his heaven. (5)

Eternal Father,
I praise you
in the silence
of the night,
made holy
made bright
with your presence.
In the bustle of the day
heated by too many activities
you are the cool shade
of peace
and quiet tranquillity,
a holy stillness,
wholly still
yet disturbing and
ruffling
my complacency.
In your cosmic silence,
deep within the deepest
part of me,
once more
I am made whole
and recreated.
Amen.

Lonely

> ... there is a desolate space within,
> a desert place whose silence is
> shouting out my loneliness and
> whose echo ever returns the
> mocking cry,
> 'No one there!' ...

> 'You are never less idle
> than when you are wholly idle,'
> observed Marcus Tullius Cicero some years ago
> in the first century BC,
> and delighting as usual in paradox,
> 'you are never less alone
> than when you are wholly alone.' (6)

As Cicero might be the first to agree, however, there is a world of difference between being alone and being lonely. Loneliness can be at its most anguished and acute when experienced in the midst of people, whether on a crowded housing estate or in a home, at work, in a large party or an intimate gathering.

Were there ever more lonely people than there seem to be now in our crowded world?

I shall never forget the noisy school trip I once saw on an island off the coast of Wales, with the cheerily squabbling and excited children in a great clump being shepherded by their teachers.

On the outskirts and separated from the others, though, walked a young girl. Outwardly nothing seemed to single her out as not fitting in with the rest, but the space around her seemed to reflect the desperate isolation and desolation of loneliness which her expression told was within her. The contrast between her and the others made my heart ache, and I longed to be able to take away her pain and make her smile again.

Another place, another memory; this time of an old man. I was waiting at traffic lights and a hearse drew up beside me.

All alone in the back seat of the one car that followed, face frozen into stricken grief, was the lone mourner. I wondered, was it his beloved wife whose coffin he was following and whose funeral he was on the way to? Why were there no other mourners, and what would be his future now that his dear companion of a lifetime was no longer with him? Then the hearse and the following car with its sad cargo moved off, and I never saw him again.

I shall never know the answer to my questions, nor even whether I had guessed correctly. But sixteen years have passed, and the stark loneliness etched on his face remains imprinted on my mind still. As does that of the young girl on the school trip: when I think of her as an adult now, I wonder – is she still lonely?

The world is so full of busy, bustling people rushing around intent on their business and activities and who, if you asked them, would probably declare fervently that they would love a bit of space, a bit of aloneness, a respite from it all, yet who you suspect might find it very daunting and threatening if they found themselves with too much of it.

I remember the clever sketch I once saw of a megastar of the early cinema screen, who simultaneously sought solitude and yet at the same time courted publicity. It depicted her standing in an open-topped car being driven down a deserted street. She has a megaphone in her hand through which she is declaiming, 'I want to be alone!' She is not alone in her confusion.

As families split and divide, then split and divide again, the traditional structures and frameworks and wider context against which people defined their identity and picture of themselves are often not there. The question, 'Who am I?' never gets a proper answer and so, when the crowd, or busyness, does not fill the gap there is an emptiness, a void, into which loneliness can too easily creep.

Society no longer trains us to be alone, nor provides us with the resources to use it creatively when we do experience it. Those who actually choose to be alone are usually looked at askance, and thought of as being a little odd.

I wonder, because we can be suspicious of aloneness are we also too often wary of another's loneliness? Can it, perhaps, be too close for comfort to our fears of what might happen to us, or even be within us already? Confronting their loneliness might confront us with our own; doubly isolated then, the lonely suffer doubly.

Jesus knew about aloneness, which he often sought as balance from the pressing crowds and in order to be alone with the Father.

However, he must also have known all about being lonely too: for example, when the disciples ran away and left him when the soldiers came to arrest him; and when he experienced the desolation of thinking, as he hung on the cross, that the Father, so constant in his presence until then, had deserted him (Matthew 26:56 and 27:46).

I wonder, was he, in fact, in some ways one of the loneliest humans who has ever lived on earth?

I can think of nothing more lonely than to know the truth of something, to feel its truth passionately with every fibre of your being, but for no one else to know it or to feel it as you do. Was that how it was for him? (cf Mark 9:19).

Even at the Last Supper, on the night before he was

crucified, it was apparent that the disciples, his constant companions throughout his public ministry, had not fully understood all that Jesus had spent the previous years trying to teach them. Any lesser person would have despaired at that moment, but Jesus never gave up hoping and believing in them, and in the grace of the Father working in their hearts, transforming what was not into what would be.

The Saviour, who knew the depths of loneliness in his earthly life, is our constant companion through his Spirit – but *especially* when we are lonely or despairing in any way; for where our need is the greatest, there he is most able to enter in.

> I am surrounded by people,
> Lord,
> but there is a desolate space within,
> a desert place whose silence is
> shouting out my loneliness and
> whose echo ever returns the
> mocking cry,
> 'No one there!
> No one who cares
> how you feel!'
>
> You who knew the utter loneliness,
> Lord,
> of the desertion of friends and
> even of the Father –
> or so it seemed –
> take away mine.
> Enter into this empty space,
> this barren place.
> Fill me to the brim
> with your presence
> and your love.
> Amen.

All alone and
late at night,
standing by the shore, I
watched and listened
to the waves breaking,
advancing and retreating,
rhythmically and continually; and
in their constancy
I thought of you.
Lord,
you keep your eternal
and vigilant watch over
all your Creation.
You are
my closest companion,
nearer to me than
I am to myself, more
essential to me than
the air I breathe.

I am filled with love when God listens
to the sound of my prayer,
when he bends down to hear me,
as I call. . . . And so,
my heart, be at peace once again.
(Psalm 116:1, 2, 7)

SPACE

> God set the far flung stars in place
> and gave each one a name . . .
> You created my inmost self,
> knit me together in my mother's womb . . .
> (Psalm 147:4 and 139:13)

> Jesus is Lord. It is he by whom all things exist.
> It was he who spiralled the DNA Helix,
> who choreographed the genetic quadrille in cell division,
> who scored the hormonal symphony . . .
> He is the Sustainer of every galaxy. (7)

One of the greatest and most wonderful mysteries is how God can both be king of infinite space, and yet dwell deep within each one of us.

For many, many years there was a comfortable and total divide between God, who was unknowable and therefore unexplainable, and everything else that needed explanation.

In terms of human history, it was only a very little while ago that everyone thought the end of the world lay at the horizon; that the earth was flat, and that if you sailed too far, you would fall off into the abyss.

Now physicists talk comfortably about the limits of space and time.

> To us convinced physicists,
> the distinction between past, present and future is an illusion,
> though a persistent one. (8)

Our minds and our imaginations and our understanding are having to expand along with the ever-expanding cosmos, as quantum physicists devise their latest theories and discover yet more parts of this amazing creation. We have had to try to get our minds round concepts which are beyond space and time.

However, is that not what we have always been trying to do with regard to questions of God and of eternity? So why exactly is it that some religious people feel so threatened by the latest quantum scientific theories?

Have you ever looked up at a star-filled night sky and wondered where, exactly, God is? It is our instinct to look up when we pray, as if God resides above and apart from us, rather than being all around and intimately involved with all that he has made.

> 'Do you believe in God?' asked Fynn.
> 'Yes', said six-year-old Anna.
> 'What is God then?'
> 'He is God! . . .
> You see, Fynn, everybody has got a point of view, but Mister God hasn't. Mister God has only points *to* view.'
> Fynn puzzled over this for some time,
> before he realised what Anna was saying:
> Humanity has an infinite number of points of view, but God has an infinite number of viewing points; that means that – God is everywhere! . . .
> Anna had taken the whole idea of God
> outside the limitation of time and
> placed him firmly in the realm of eternity. (9)

Unlike six-year-old Anna, a number of adult people find it a problem to hold together the latest discoveries of science with their religious belief. However, instead of thinking that perhaps their concept of God is too small, they try to emphasise the irreconcilable difference between science and religion, and state firmly that there can be no reconciliation.

This is not the problem of the scientists, for they cannot deny their discoveries. It is the problem of narrow religious thinking, which says you can talk about one or the other, but not about one *and* the other.

There is a famous Jewish thinker and writer called Martin Buber who was always trying to get people to understand the significance of the word 'and'. He said how important it was as a link word between such words as 'I' and 'You'.

'Science' and 'Religion' could be another example.

'Empty out your teacup God', (10)

said Anthony de Mello, an Indian Jesuit who was always trying to get people to expand their concept of God.

If we did that, and then read the tea leaves, I wonder what message we would find there? Probably a heartfelt plea from God to open up our minds, our hearts, our souls to the true wonder of his glory as expressed in every aspect of his creation, and which he is revealing to us in every new and amazing and wondrous discovery that the scientists make.

> Wherever we venture you are
> there before us.
> There is no place where you
> are not.
> Only you can hold together
> the far-flung Cosmos
> and the space at
> the centre of me.

'Going where no human has ever gone before . . .' 'Star Trek', 'Babylon 5', 'Deep Space 9', 'Star Wars' . . . such TV series and films are amongst the most popular television viewing, especially amongst young people. They are growing up in a world of computers, space travel, sophisticated technology of all kinds, and frontiers of science in every direction that are constantly being extended. It is all very exciting, but it can be disconcerting for them too.

In this fast-changing world, where is the stable ground? Where are the hooking-on and fixed reference points, so needed in order to frame our understanding of who we are within this evolving world?

Never before has a faith system been more important: a concept of a loving God holding all these bewilderingly diverse fragments together.

As the frontiers of our knowledge expand, and the world with it, we must try to let our ideas and concepts of God expand as well at the same, if not at a faster, rate.

We must try to empty out our teacup God and let God expand to occupy space, and beyond.

When God led Moses and the Israelites out of Egypt and into the desert, he went before. He led them to a new understanding. Their journey was one of learning new things about themselves, the world in which they lived, and of God's relationship to both them *and* to his world. Out in that space, that open place, they were able to begin to perceive something of the vastness of God, and of his love and commitment to all that he has made.

> Deep within each one of us
> lies a space as wide
> as the world –
> and wider.
>
> How can this be?

Deep within each one of us
dwells the Lord,
the Creator
of all things.

He contains the universe in himself,
holding the space within
and the space without
in equal tension.

Thus I am
in the world and
the world is
in me.

Eternal Wisdom,
standing outside space and time,
seeing the whole story and
filling in the gaps between
past-present-future
so they become one,
you have made us
little less than gods
and entrusted your creation
into our hands.
As our brains push out
the frontiers
of our knowledge,
help our hearts
to keep pace with
the learning and to
beat out constantly
the rhythm
of universal love.
Amen.

Despairing

Joy is quiet and lives in one place,
but misery rages noisily down all the
corridors of the world. (11)

My heart was broken.
Dr Salmon mended it.
He put in the angel's wings
and now I am better. (12)

'There's a darkness in despair which – which settles like a storm cloud around your heart and mind. It shuts out all the hope and all the light.

'There's a terrible kind of loneliness. A – a – an isolation too.

'You feel – you feel – you've sunk so deep you – you can't explain how it feels.

'It just seems that everyone else can cope with life except you, and that only makes you feel even worse, and the blackness even blacker.'

Each sentence, begun hesitantly, gathered force and power as the speaker felt his way to the exact words he needed in order to express what he wanted to say.

'He' was a disconcertingly articulate 13-year-old called Jason. The words described how he felt.

His small physical size belied his very adult experience and perception of the world which, he declared with some justification, had not done him many favours at all.

There is no mistaking genuine distress and despair. Jason's feelings were obviously very real, and dredged up from the deepest part of his inner being.

'When I was a kid,' he continued, 'I had a book. On the

front was a worm, and it ate its way right through the pages. That's how I feel.'

Jason's words underlined the sad fact that such feelings are not the prerogative of adults. Even the smallest of children, locked into situations over which they have no control, can know that 'darkness of despair' of Jason's vivid description.

Difficult family situations, bullying, or the inability to live up to high standards set either by themselves or others, are just a few examples. Or, maybe, no discernible explanation or reason can be identified either by the child, or by an observer; the underlying causes being too deep for easy recall or understanding.

There are so many people, of all ages, living lives of quiet desperation rather than the noisy raging of Tolstoy's description. If they did rage, perhaps the rest of us would hear and act sooner.

And if we did hear, what could we do? Doctors can provide the medical help, and a variety of social and care workers can try to alleviate the physical conditions.

But what about the rest of us?

We are all born into community, and this gives us a clear responsibility for each other's welfare. Ancient communities understood this very well. They knew the good of the individual affects the wellbeing of the group. In the Old Testament, clear rules were laid down for the treatment and care of all the vulnerable, whoever they were.

Despair isolates. Also, with the build-up of despair there is a parallel draining away of the energy required to change the situation. Or, maybe, previous attempts to change those things perceived as causing the problem have met with little or no success and so, eventually, an exhausted apathy sets in: a kind of mind-numbness which coats and shields too-raw feelings from any more pain. It is difficult to stop yourself feeling anything, yet still be movitated enough to take action.

It is so important that those caught up in the 'darkness of despair' are able to find someone with whom to share their feelings: a doctor, a teacher or another professional helper, or a trusted neighbour or friend – to 'speak' the grief that lies within.

Sometimes, in the very act of sharing, a pathway of understanding opens up for the person, and they can then find their own solution. So we must each try to be attentive to the hint dropped or the unexpressed need which may, nevertheless, be written plain on face or in body language.

> The grief that cannot speak
> whispers the o'erfraught heart
> and bids it break. (13)

As I write this, Nelson Mandela is in town and every area of English life is vying and competing with each other to demonstrate their deep admiration for this most wonderful man.

Twenty-seven years of imprisonment on the notorious Robben Island has not destroyed his hope. Somehow he managed not to give way to despair. He has a great sense of destiny it seems, of being a part of something so much greater than just himself, that his time in jail was a part of the long road to freedom for his people, of being able to take the most negative situations and somehow turn them round for good.

It is so easy to set such people apart as being different from us, but Nelson Mandela *is* just like us: a human being, and one, I am sure, who did feel despairing at times. But I imagine he faced it and looked it in the eye, so to speak, named it, and then went on in God's strength.

> Hold up
> your despair
> and place it
> in God's care.

I think of Jason, and I hope and pray that his imagination is caught up and fired by this man and his enduring hope even when everything seemed hopeless; that he will be inspired by Nelson Mandela's example not to let despair destroy his potential and stop him becoming the man he is intended to be.

'Never give up, not whilst you have one speck of life left in you', declared Jamie, the courageous young girl who captured the hearts of so many, and who eventually died of leukaemia, but who lived life fully and victoriously to the last days.

Jesus saw the world of various need, beneath the surface expression of despair, in the globe his Father held in the palm of his hand:

'Let me go to them', he said.

> From the highest
> transcendence
> to the most intimate
> immanence,
> you
> plunged through the fabric
> of society's mores
> – and lesses –
> not stopping
> until you came to
> rest for a while at
> the very entrance to
> hell,

around whose gateway gather
the down in the depths
and those who
are out to get
a quick buck
from them.
In just the same
way as
– once and for all –
you
ripped the Temple
curtain in two,
letting
your love
burst out
to
embrace
the
world.

When I said, 'my foot is slipping'
your love, O Lord, supported me.
When anxiety was great within me
your consolation brought joy to my soul . . .
The Lord has become my fortress, and my God
the rock in which I take refuge.
(Psalm 94:18, 19, 22)

WONDER

A wonder am I,
and all your works are wonders.
(Psalm 139:14)

Two things fill my mind with ever-increasing wonder
and awe . . . the starry heavens above me
and the moral law within me. (14)

Young Albert was a great worry to his parents.

They feared he might be backward. He was three before he uttered a word, was a quiet and dreamy lad, and did not like the usual boyhood pursuits.

When he was four years old he fell ill, and was confined to bed. In order to help him pass the time, his father gave him an electric compass.

Albert Einstein was fascinated with the way the compass needle was always drawn to the north. The mystery of it fired his imagination, and triggered off a lifelong passionate curiosity with the unexplained in the universe.

There was a childlike quality to Einstein's wonder that he retained throughout his life, and which enabled him to ask the questions which it had not occurred to anyone else to ask. It probably also helped him to produce his general theory of relativity in 1915, thereby providing the cosmological framework for most of twentieth-century physics.

Anyone who has regular dealings with children knows their insatiable curiosity. Their favourite word is 'why'?

Watch a child totally caught up in the wonder of a spider's

web, or the pattern of frost on a window pane, or any of the other million miracles they see in a day.

Enter into a child's wonder, and you enter into another world inhabited by breathtaking things and happenings. The ordinary, the everyday, is transformed into the extraordinary, the out-of-this-world. And they are so observant and appreciative of detail that the average adult just would not see. Small wonder then that Jesus used children to illustrate qualities that we should retain when we grow up.

In his book, *One Minute Wisdom,* Anthony de Mello recounts the following tale:

> The Haji who lived at the outskirts of the town was said to perform miracles, so his home was a centre of pigrimage for large crowds of sick people.
>
> The Master, who was known to be quite uninterested in the miraculous, would never reply to questions on the Haji.
>
> When asked point blank why he was opposed to miracles, he replied, 'How can one be opposed to what is taking place before one's eyes each moment of the day?' (15)

When we reach adulthood, the wondering and the questions should not stop. We should always be changing the statements in our lives so that they ask questions; taking what has happened, questioning it, and converting it into living.

God is the great questioner, and he will press his questions on us. He will not leave us in peace until we address them and try to find the answers. This is part of our pilgrimage, of our journeying towards him, and how we grow spiritually.

'We must reason together',

said Isaiah, so reminding us our questions must be meaningful in order that we can use the answers in the reality of our lives. We should question things, and we should question people.

> Look around you – there are people around you.
> Maybe you will remember one of them all your life
> and later eat your heart out because you
> didn't make use of the opportunity
> to ask him or her questions. (16)

So said Alexander Solzhenitsyn, one of the great questioners of Communism, who wrote many very powerful books based on the consequences of this particular political philosophy on people's lives.

When our God-given intellect to reason and to discern and to discover is held together with a childlike wonder and respect for what is being unfolded before our eyes; when the revelations of both head and heart are allowed to synthesise and become one, then, truly, we will see miracles.

It is said that we have within ourselves the answer to every question we may wish to ask – if only we knew how to look for it.

I don't know about you, but I find *that* the most awesome and miraculous thing there could ever be to wonder about.

> It is said, Lord, that
> within me are all
> the answers to all the
> questions ever asked anywhere
> and by anyone.

But how can this be?
They must be buried so
very deep and totally
inaccessible to me.
I've thought and
thought, Lord, till
my head is spinning.
About to give up in
despair it suddenly came
– inspirationally? –
down at the very
depth, the very heart
and central core of
my being, is where
you dwell.
You have all the answers
to anything I may ever
think to ask.
But you do it
by responding
'Why?'
and
'What do you really want?'

Oh!

Wondrous God!

Most holy and wondrous God!

Where are the words
to declare what
I long to say?
I struggle to reach them but
they are not there.

The greatest praise,
I conclude,
is an empty page
with nothing inscribed.

For you are

beyond

description.

Amen.

Loss and Gain

Too Young to Die

October 21 1966: – 116 children died
when a slag heap collapsed on
the Pantglas Primary School, Aberfan, in Wales.

March 13 1996: – 16 children died
when a gunman opened fire on them at
the Dunblane Primary School, in Scotland.

Why, God!
Why did their
child have
to die?

Cry, Child!
Cry, for I too
weep at what
was done.

In Wales, sheep graze on the grassy hillside that has replaced the tip. The children's graves nearby, in two neat rows, are beautifully and lovingly tended.

In Scotland, two days after the killings, there is no other focus as yet, save the gymnasium where the slaughter took place. Flowers, stacked high on the school threshold, and from young and old, bear messages that reflect the pain, fear and bewilderment of those who gave them.

'Why?'
'Too young'
– are the two most oft-repeated.

Politicians of all persuasions mercifully, for once, do not try to outdo each other; their stumbling offerings of sadness and sympathy have much more dignity than many of their more usual well-oiled and well-turned phrases.

A childhood death can rarely be anything other than devastating for those who are left contemplating that most precious space which the child once occupied.

Going for a meal for the first time with a couple with whom I had only recently become acquainted, I picked up a photo of a bright-eyed lad of about 7 years. His suppressed energy seemed to bubble out of the picture.

'Is this your son?' I asked.

'Yes', the father replied, with a tender and wistful smile. 'That's Sam. He died, eleven years ago, after a simple operation went wrong. It was very sudden. He was six years old.'

As the evening progressed, the conversation turned once more to Sam. His parents shared how, although he is and would always be in their minds and hearts, the terrible, tearing and constant pain of loss had slowly given way to a deep thanksgiving for those six brief years, during which he had brought so much joy into their lives.

However, the sharp stabs of longing, there at expected times such as Christmas and birthdays, would strike at unexpected moments too, triggered by often small things: the sound of a piece of music; the sight of a football scarf of his favourite team; his favourite colour; or the knowledge of his peer group, now in their latter teens dating and partying or planning for adventurous trips and university, but with Sam no longer in their midst.

His sister and brother are both older than he. They still feel displaced in the family hierarchy; particularly the one who was the middle of three and who is now the youngest.

'The gap will never be filled, and nor would we wish to fill it', Sam's mother concluded. 'For us, Sam still lives, both in our hearts and in our memories, and yet also in another place. And, one day, I shall hold my son again. I know it.'

A faith that has the faith to look through death.

The disciples came to Jesus and asked, 'Who is the greatest in the kingdom of heaven?'
So he called a little child to him whom he set among them. Then he said:
'In truth I tell you, unless you change
and become like little children
you will never enter the kingdom of Heaven.
And so, the one who makes himself as little
as this little child
is the greatest in the kingdom of Heaven.'
(Matthew 18:1-4)

Now and then in life,
Lord Jesus,
we come face to face with
tragic,
early,
violent
death.

You raised
Jairus's daughter,
and Lazarus,
and the son
of the widow
and so many others,
I'm sure, of whom
we have not heard.

I want to pray now,
Lord,
for all who have died
too young in years.
Draw near
to those who grieve
so terribly
at their passing.

Raise them up
from the tomb
of their despair.

Amen.

Postscript:
Friday, 22 March 1996

The funerals of the sixteen children, and of their teacher who died defending them, have taken place.
The evening news on the television brought the following interview from the Headmaster of the Dunblane Primary School:
'Today, the children of Dunblane Primary School returned . . .
'As I walked around the school this morning, I came across a group of children laughing and joking together.
'I rounded a corner, and two more were arguing.
'We are returning to normality.
'The evil that visited this place has gone.'

Wednesday, 9 October 1996

During the Memorial Service for the children and their teacher in Dunblane, in his sermon the Minister declared:
'Darkness cannot be allowed to be the last word.'

And so, Lord,
your healing work goes on.
Gently, tenderly, patiently, you continue
to gather up the broken hearts
and graft them into your own.

Your life blood, flowing into
those deadened with grief,
soothing the ache,
washing away the pain
and releasing the grip
of distress and anguish.

O Heart,
residing within the heart of
all who grieve
and whispering,
'Be at peace once again.'

LETTING GO

> If I have freedom in my love,
> And in my soul am free;
> Angels alone that soar above,
> Enjoy such liberty. (17)

> In the letting go we find life;
> for deeper than the striving is the flowing,
> deeper than the searching is the knowing
> and deeper than the grieving is the mystery,
> in which darkness and light are one. (18)

I have a great-aunt of over one hundred years of age who, because of failing eyesight, recently decided to give all her beloved craft books to a Hospice for the use of the patients there.

It was the next stage of 'getting her house in order'. Previous stages have included sorting through old photographs, and then giving the majority away to the appropriate people.

She still crochets busily however, relying, though, more on touch than on vision. She lives with her sister of over ninety years, who looks after her, drives the car, talks knowledgeably about camshafts and injection systems, and who does not look a day over an elegant eighty.

When you go there for tea, there is always a wide selection of cakes, and the older aunt keeps a hawk-like eye on your teacup in order to ensure it is never empty.

My grandmother, their elder sister, died at the relatively tender age of ninety-one years.

About two years before her death, she declared calmly that she was ready to die.

She had spent part of her married life in the tropics in a remote jungle area in Madagascar with my missionary grandfather, where she had survived many attacks of malaria, had given birth to, and had raised, four daughters until they were sent to boarding school in England, and had set up and run what must have been one of the first fair trading schemes ever, anywhere, for the local women: first teaching herself to make lace, and then teaching the craft to the local women for them to make and to sell.

Subsequently, she had coped with, and overcome, many vicissitudes, but she never stopped dancing with life. When too old to do it physically, her eyes still danced, and she would often have tears of laughter running down her cheeks.

Now, however, she felt ready to let go her tenacious grip on life.

'The trouble is,' my grandmother added after a moment's pause, I just cannot get out of the habit of living.'

This ability to celebrate life and yet, at the same time, to be perfectly ready to let it go into the hands of the Creator who first gave it, is an enviable balance.

Is it, maybe, a gift given only to those who have lived life – however long or short – fully and with the whole of their hearts, so that, when God reaches out for the loan of life to be returned, they are able to surrender it graciously and freely?

If so, there is a paradox here, as there is in so much of life.

Letting go can be hard, and it can be frightening. It can be especially daunting and difficult when it is some one, or thing, that has helped to frame our understanding of who we are as a person. However, the time may come when holding on is no longer appropriate, and we are called on to let go in order that we may move on to new opportunities and the developing of new potential.

The Story of the Rich Young Ruler that Jesus told illustrates this. He is possessed by his wealth; his money frames his understanding of who he is. Jesus, as he so often does, challenges at the young man's weak point.

Like a two-edged sword going between joint and marrow, Jesus goes to the heart of the matter. You may be obeying all of the Commandments, he tells him, but there is something else holding you back – your love of your money. And so, you should give it away:

> Sell everything you own and
> distribute the money to the poor,
> and you will have treasure in heaven;
> then come, follow me.
> (Luke 18:18f.)

Like the rich young ruler we may need to let go of something, or someone, into the past, before we can embrace what the future may bring.

Perhaps, then, we need to practise developing a light touch right across our lives so that, when we are called upon to release our hold at some point, we are able to do it in a way which celebrates not only what has been, but also what is to be.

Balance is the ability to celebrate what is, and yet not to mourn what is not; to aim to be as content to be without, as to be with.

It is a letting go into freedom.

> The parent birds had nurtured and fed their young
> until they were strong and grown and, now,
> it was time for their offspring to leave.

Watching from below, I could imagine how the young birds might be feeling as they teetered on the edge of the nest.

Behind them the security, the warmth,
the care they had always known.

In front of them the beckoning world, full of new things.
But, in order to experience it, they would
have to let go of that
which contained the past.
In order to fly,
they had first to leave the nest.

Perhaps they would never have done it
had not their mother, instinctively wise,
given each an encouraging little push.
One by one, they fell out of the nest
and began to plummet towards the ground.

Then, at that heartstopping point
when it seemed certain they would be dashed
to death on the ground,
each discovered their wings and found they could fly –
and soared into the sky.

My grandmother had only one request for her funeral:
that the following hymn be sung –

O Love that wilt not let me go,
I rest my weary soul in thee:
I give thee back the life I owe,
That in thine ocean depths its flow
May richer, fuller, be.

O Light that followest all my way,
I yield my flickering torch to thee:
My heart restores its borrowed ray,
That in thy sunshine's blaze its day
May brighter, fairer be.

O Joy that seekest me through pain,
 I cannot close my heart to thee:
I trace the rainbow through the rain,
 And feel the promise is not vain
  That morn should tearless be.

O Cross that liftest up my head,
 I dare not ask to fly from thee:
I lay in dust life's glory dead,
And from the ground there blossoms red
 Life that shall endless be. (19)

Loss

> For death and life, in ceaseless strife,
> beat wild on this earth's shore,
> and all our calm is in that balm –
> not lost but gone before. (20)

The gradual loss of a loved one through physical illness is always hard to bear; especially in situations where you are unable to relieve the suffering and are only able to be alongside, offering your constancy and your care.

You see that cherished person progressively weaken and become more limited in his or her activity, and know that the situation will only end with death.

However, there is a *particular* anguish in watching a much-loved one apparently disintegrate mentally and emotionally before your eyes; to see the doors of communication close one by one, and the shutters put up against the windows of their mind and personality; to be unable to know what thinking, if any, lies behind the blank gaze; whether your words hold any meaning for them or, indeed, whether *you* hold any meaning for them; not to know whether they even recognise you as their friend, sibling, life partner or child.

Dad –
    Once – it was your mother who patiently spooned food
               into your mouth, and you
        who spat out what you did not like.
    Then – it was you who patiently spooned food into my mouth,
          and I who spat out what I did not like.
        Now – it is I who patiently spoon food into
              your mouth, and you
       who dribble out what you do not like.

The circle has been completed.
The end has joined the beginning.
Dusk has met the dawn.
There is a poignant anguish in this
inverted parent-child relationship:
what you once did for me, now I
do for you; tenderly, respectfully,
and with a sense of awe.
Personal tasks. Intimate tasks.

And I wonder –
Do you know?
Do you mind?
Do you care?
Behind that blank stare
do you know it is me?

Visiting round the geriatric ward one day, I stopped beside the bed of an elderly man who lay there, motionless. His wife sat beside him, holding his hand and stroking it.

She was talking softly to him, her tone loving and gentle, although she was getting no response. He gazed blankly past her, into some distant place and time.

'He likes to hear all the news about everyone and everything', she said, smiling at me. 'People think I am daft, and say he can't understand – but how do they *know?* Brains are such complicated things aren't they. Just because one part has gone doesn't mean that none of it works. You are encouraged to speak to people who are in comas. What's the difference?

'I believe that at some deep level of his mind my words do find a home, and that he understands in his own way. He was such a dear, handsome, man. I know he doesn't look it or seem it now to some. But, to me, he will always be wonderful. This dementia thing is only a surface covering. I see him as he really is, deep down; as I know God sees him.

'So, yes dear. I would like you to say a prayer, please. Say it for him, to him. He'd like that.'

> God does not see as human beings see;
> they look at appearances but God looks at the heart.
> (1 Samuel 16:7)

There is a poem, called 'A Crabbit Old Woman', which was found among the possessions of an old lady in a geriatric ward after her death. Since then I should think there can only be a few hospitals which have not had it pinned to their noticeboards as a poignant reminder that appearances do not necessarily reflect the reality inside.

It begins, 'What do you see, nurses, what do you see? What are you thinking when you look at me? A crabbit old woman, not very wise, who dribbles her food and makes no reply . . .' and continues with a journey down her memories of childhood and teens, marriage and children, grandchildren and widowhood, to old age and infirmity.

It concludes, '. . . But inside this old carcass a young girl still dwells, and now and again my battered heart swells. I remember the joys, I remember the pain, and I'm loving and living life over again . . . Open your eyes, open and see – not a crabbit old woman. Look closer. See me.' (21)

In our achievement-orientated society, someone who has not the ability to learn to read, or write, or cross the road – who can't climb the ladder of self-sufficiency – or whose mental faculties for some reason or another have degenerated, is sometimes an affront. It is as if he or she tugs at the very foundation of our accepted values, and the things we pursue and strive after.

And yet, Jesus said:

> 'In as much as you welcome the least
> of my brothers and sisters,
> you welcome me.'
> (Matthew 25:40)

Jesus welcomes and affirms, and sets special value on, the person who is weak in the eyes of the world, and assures us they are the specially beloved of God.

Some years later, St. Paul was to write:

> 'It is precisely the parts of the body
> that seem to be the weakest
> which are, in fact, the indispensable ones . . .
> Each part is to be equally concerned for all the others.
> If one part is hurt, all parts share its pain.'
> (1 Corinthians 12:22f.)

There is an African proverb, 'When the foot gets a thorn in it, the whole body must stoop to pull it out.' What happens to one part of the body intimately affects the rest of it. If the thorn is ignored, the wound will fester, and affect the whole body.

So, when we acknowledge and act upon our responsibility towards the vulnerable in our midst, we learn something so important. We begin to learn that in sharing their lives and sufferings – sharing in a way that lets the other person give to us – sharing in a way that learns to welcome what society too often sees as weakness or a source of embarrassment or shame as, in fact, a source of life – then something radical happens to us.

In a very deep sense, will we not then begin to learn what it is to belong to each other – and to form a body that has the mystery of Jesus hidden within it, and within the hearts of each of us?

Father –
Not 'mentally disabled' but
'mentally differently abled':
I used to think these were
semantic niceties, modern
and politically correct.
Older, humbler, wiser now
I know better.
There is a deep mystery
in the withdrawal of a person
to the centre of their being –
where you dwell.

Forgive me when I judge and value
by appearances,
for appearances can too often deceive.
Teach me to look at each
person I meet with
Christ-eyes –
and to love with a
Christ-heart.
Amen.

When I visit the bereaved, or take funerals, a favourite prayer for me to use is from *The Dream of Gerontius*. I think it is profoundly moving and most beautiful, and those who hear it seem to share my feeling about it.

Go forth upon your journey, Christian soul,
go from this world.
Go in the name of God the Omnipotent Father,
who created you.
Go in the name of Jesus Christ our Lord, who died for you.
Go in the name of the Holy Spirit,
who has been poured out on you,
and will sustain us both until we meet again.
May God be with you till we meet again. (22)

New Experiences

> All experience is an arch wherethro'
> gleams that untravelled world whose margin
> fades for ever and ever when I move . . . (23)

In the dawning of Creation, when
the world was coming to birth
– that ultimate example of new experiences –
was it new,
God,
even for you?

Or had you
– and this is a serious theological question –
seen it all before?
And so was the Big Bang as
anticlimactic for you
as a party-popper?

The Malagasi people have the greatest respect and awe for the chameleon, to which they ascribe divine powers. They believe that the chameleon's independently swivelling eyes enable it to keep one eye on the past, and the other on the future . . .

Mystic Meg; Crystal Balls; Tarot Cards; Tea-leaves; the Stars . . .

The future has always fascinated humankind, it seems. And trying to find out what it holds in store preoccupies many. Yet, I wonder, wouldn't knowing it for sure take all the mystery, the excitement, the curiosity, out of life?

Adventure, or exploring the unknown, would no longer be an option, for there would be no unknown to explore.

Perhaps, if I had realised the extent of the danger of what turned out in fact to be one of the peak experiences, one of the great thrills, of my life I would not have attempted it in the first place:

High in the mountains of Slovenia, to the north of former Yugoslavia, is one of the world championship white-water rafting runs.

How I came to be one of the ten who set out to run the course that day would take too long to recount here. Suffice it to say I was there and clad, like the others, in wet suit, helmet, and with bare feet pushed into the leather thongs attached to the raft floor. We perched around the outer rim, each armed with a paddle, and at the back stood the leader, Stefan, with the fixed long steering oar. The sun was hot, but the water, as I had found when we launched the raft, was ice-cold.

The first few minutes we paddled through very choppy water, with mountains rising high on either side, and negotiated a few rocks, but it all seemed a bit tame compared with the photos I had been shown, and I felt disappointed. Then we emerged into a wide open, curiously still lake, and headed for a narrow opening on the other side.

Leaving the lake was like dropping from a millpond into a cauldron of boiling, seething water. The river dropped at a steep angle and the mountains, towering on either side, whipped by at a giddy speed. Great clumps of jagged rocks barred our path and we weaved around them, or through them, as was most appropriate or just possible. Stefan shouted instructions from the back, and we reacted accordingly; sometimes paddling furiously, sometimes one side or another dragging paddles, or stopping paddling altogether.

The raft, meanwhile, plunged, tilted at crazy angles, regularly spun full round, bounded off the visible rocks, and scraped over the invisible ones but, miraculously, did not turn over.

Equally miraculously, no one fell out. If they had, that would have been it. No one could have survived for more than a few moments in that tempestuous torrent. The reason for the bare feet in the thongs was apparent: they were our anchors, essential to our survival. How Stefan kept his balance was a mystery. Through the blinding spray, you could see him straining to keep the long oar from being wrenched from his hands.

The passage of time became meaningless. The experience of each moment, and the concentration required, was so intense that we were totally in the present. On and on we rocketed.

Then, suddenly, we had come to the end of the run, and the steep mountain torrent quickly levelled out.

It had been wonderful, and truly one of the peak experiences of my life. I had loved every minute of it. Rarely have I felt such a rush of disappointment at the finish of something: the contrast of the torrent with the still water mirrored exactly how I felt.

It was only then I remembered my fear of deep water, which I had had since I nearly drowned when I was fifteen years of age.

Two things had been achieved that day; the holding-back power of a negative experience from the past had been greatly diminished, and I had learned something more of the exhilaration felt by intimately encountering, and becoming one with, yet another aspect of God's amazing and wonderfully diverse Creation.

In *Brave New World* by Aldous Huxley, and more recently Dennis Potter's *Cold Lazarus*, the authors each draw their own picture of a fearsome world where everything is controlled; by computers, by people with the power of gods, or by budgets, and all the precious spontaneity and freedom of individual expression and curiosity is treated with the deepest suspicion. Yet, in each story, there are still people – now on the outskirts of those societies – who are passionately committed to restoring a world where people were allowed to feel as God had created them to feel.

The search for new experiences does have its down side, when it is merely a search for a quick buzz, a quick fix of adrenaline: when its result is a diminution of our precious God-given freedom to control our own lives, and when it makes us less human than we were before. Many things in our modern society come into that category.

However, our modern society also presents us with opportunities undreamed of by most of our ancestors to experience different and new aspects of this wonderful world, and of ourselves.

The choice, and the responsibility, is ours as to what we do with the opportunities placed before us.

> I asked a question at the beginning,
> Lord,
> but I think I knew the answer
> even then
> – inasmuch as I can ever know your mind –
> I believe that
> you
> rejoice at each new happening
> with us,
> our excitement, our joy, is yours
> as our pain is yours.
> You feel it as we do,
> because you enter
> into the deepest part
> – the deepest heart –
> of it
> *all.*

Each new day
that dawns,
full of fresh promise,
speaks of your
soft breath,
caressing touch
and divine gifting.
Help me, Lord,
to experience it
with all the wonder,
the breath-held
excitement and
anticipation
of a child on
their birthday morning.
Amen.

Unemployed

When the path of life is steep,
keep your mind even. (24)

'Redundant':

The word resonates with the sense of being surplus to requirement; a non-essential person in worldly estimation.

Sadly, it is now used to describe such a range of situations that, like so many other formerly powerful words, it has been devalued; its ability to set us back on our heels has been neutralised.

Yet, the short statement: 'You are redundant', has huge implications for the recipient, and embodies a world turned upside down.

'When I first heard I was to be made redundant,' he said, 'I was very shocked, as it was so totally unexpected. I thought my job was essential, and so was secure. But now I know that was a comfortable illusion. The reality is different: there is no such thing as an indispensable person.

'The routine that framed my daily life has gone. I feel useless. And I feel I no longer fit into society where, nor in the way, I did. My confidence is at zero point.

'In fact, I feel like an outcast.

'I had to leave almost immediately. I was not given an opportunity to clear my desk, or to go around saying my farewells. Of course, there was no leaving present or party. It's not that I wanted a lot of razzmatazz, but I feel there is so much unfinished personal and social business.

'It made me feel that I was at fault in some way, being treated like that. Whereas, in fact, I had served that company for many years faithfully, and to the best of my ability.

'I'm not the only one, I'm sad to say', he continued. 'Others were made redundant at the same time, as well. Many of us now feel like a non-person, instead of someone of value and valued. We made a good team. Mutually supportive, and loyal to each other, and to the firm. How can you value that in monetary terms?

'At least I can console myself I have had a job. At least I know what it is to work, the satisfaction – and the money! – that you have at the end of the working week; which is more than many of our school-leavers, and university-leavers, can say. I guess that theirs is the worse sadness, for they have never known the affirmation and sense of pride in a job of work well done.'

'By any other name' (Tune: Tolling bell)

I   re-rating (your future)

A   restructuring
M   reshaping

S   realignment (organisational)
O   re-engineering (business process)
R   rearrangement initiatives (production schedule)
R   downsizing
Y   de-layering

Y   rationalising
O   streamlining
U   flattening organisational structures
R   radically examining overheads
E   refocusing strategic direction

U meeting market imperatives
N concentrating on core activities
E being given a career opportunity
M being helped out of a rut
P being offered a career realignment scheme
L intensely competitive markets
O increasing capital effectiveness
Y intensified productivity drives
E offering personal premature exit agreements.
D – Goodbye. (25)

      Outcast
    from society,
      cast out
    from society,
     struggling
    to bring the
      light of
understanding and
      love, a
    New Order,
      into a
       dark,
       alien
       and
       lost
      world:
    a King in
  lowly disguise
       so
   you'd know
      what
     it's like.

Help me, Lord!
The day stretches ahead
long and empty,
and I feel my confidence
and my hope
ebbing away
each new day that passes.

I have so much to offer –

I know it's true
that to you
I am of
infinite value

But it doesn't feel
that way
to
me.

Amen.

In Kingdom estimation there is no such being as a non-essential person, for, in the sight of God, each one of us is unique and precious.

Our value to God – thank God! – is not measured in terms of our market value.

The Parable of the Labourers in the Vineyard (Matthew 20:1f) is as applicable to those who are unable to find work, for whatever reason, as to those who find employment:

Right up to the eleventh hour,
the owner of the vineyard went out to the market place,
found men standing around hoping for work,
and employed them.

Presumably, though, yet others were not so fortunate that day, and they remained 'surplus to requirement'. Did they too know the great courage, the teeth-gritted determination, required to continue to seek work even when you are continually turned away, which is so much the common experience of those who seek work today?

Did they manage to be sustained by the thought that there was always the next day?

Perhaps, then, their luck would change, and they would be offered work. But it was so important they did not give up hope, and that despair did not stop them from making themselves available any more, for then the owner of the vineyard would not have found them.

> Jesus,
> you were a special friend
> to those who felt
> cast-down
> or
> cast-out
> by society.
> May all who feel rejected
> by the work-world
> know that friendship today,
> accepting and valuing them
> for what they are,
> not for their economic
> viability.
> Amen.

> What shall be tomorrow,
> think not of asking;
> each day that fortune gives you,
> be it what it may,
> set down for gain. (26)

WORK

God be in my week, and in my working.

Spirituality is not apart from our daily lives;
it *is* our daily lives. (27)

After a lazy and relaxing – or at least different pace and tempo – day off, and as our thoughts turn towards the coming week, many of us must wonder, 'How can I keep some essence of this experience of peace, and of the closeness of God's presence, in my everyday working life?'

Days off are precious times when, hopefully, we are able to restore some of the balance and sense of inner stillness and peace and wellbeing, which may have been diminished through the previous days.

It is so easy for all this to be lost once more when the phone is constantly ringing, the demands of the job seem to be ever-mounting, and the pile of work seems never to diminish, however much we apply ourselves.

So, where on earth is God in all this busyness?

It is a great temptation, isn't it, to 'overcome' this problem by making a mental divide between spirituality and work. Religion is for Sundays, and work, with, perhaps, an alternative set of ethics, is for Mondays to Fridays.

Alan Ecclestone, however, an Anglican priest who spent most of his working life amongst the steelmills of Sheffield, saw this kind of division as totally un-Christian. It was one of his favourite themes, and a subject on which he preached many times.

All of life is spiritual, for all is part of God's creation.
There is no divide between sacred and secular,
work and worship, religion and politics . . .

Spirituality is not apart from our daily lives;
it *is* our daily lives.
But it is a life with a cutting edge,
not avoiding the pain or the fear . . .

. . . A new look at the ground we stand on
is always a 'must'
if we are to know ourselves in the presence of God
in the factory, the laboratory,
the farm, the city:
all of which have their particular
problems of right usage
and ultimate purpose. (28)

Spirituality is the process of drawing *all* areas of our life and experience and activity into the holy or spiritual dimension, and thus into God's healing and unifying presence.

God continues to re-create and restore his creation, and we are called to be co-creators with him. Work is one way we can participate in this activity.

For the unemployed, work is seen as a blessing. For many at work though, the pressures can make it seem like a punishment.

How can we begin to reconcile such polarised views?

Much traditional Christian teaching – Brother Lawrence, a Carmelite lay Brother, and Saint Thérèse of Lisieux, are just two examples – has suggested we 'do our work for God'.

However, there is a danger in this approach in that it can

devalue work, and encourage an attitude of 'grin and bear it'.

Perhaps, then, should we not rather be seeking to 'do it *with* God'; bringing God into the very centre of our activities, as work companion and intimate colleague? – As the One with whom we are continually conducting an inner dialogue, and from whom we can be constantly drawing sustenance and strength?

In this way we will be blessing the workplace as well, by drawing his mysterious and mighty healing presence into the very centre of the everyday work-world – where it is so desperately needed.

> God,
> be in my week
> and in my working
>
> God,
> be in my relationships
> and in my relating
> God,
> be in my leisure
> and in my relaxing
> God,
> may there be
> no place where you are not.
> Amen.

LORD,
when I look around the world of work,
and see the dissolution of former certainties,
the increasing competition for diminishing work,
the low morale of those seeking work and not finding it,
the disputes over short-term contracts,
and the fragmentation of people trying to cope with
increased work-loads:
so much change in such a short space of time –
it is easy to feel disheartened.

So, Lord, where are you in all of this?

Can you possibly be found in this frenetic workplace
and, if so,
what disguise are you wearing?
Is it the clown's mask
of those of us foolish enough to
work under such pressure?

Does Easter hold the answer, I wonder?

I think of Palm Sunday,
with its feel-good factor and sense of certainty
about what the future has to hold;
through the events of Holy Week, as the
clouds thickened and darkened around that increasingly
solitary figure,
to Good Friday,
when you mounted your Cross
and burned your imprint for ever into all situations
of pain
or despair
or confusion . . .

But that's not where the story ends,
is it, Lord,
for no tomb could hold you in.
Once again,
you were immediately back at work,
reclaiming lost souls,
bringing hope
into places where formerly
hopelessness reigned.
And that was even before
Easter Day
had dawned, and
you
declared yourself risen.

I wonder, Lord,
is that your task for me?
To be busy about
the marketplace of life,
reclaiming souls lost
in a world
of discouragement,
or stress,
or uncertainty?
Am I to be
an Easter Day person
in other people's
Good Friday world?

Caught and Held

Addicted

*'Me? I'm not addicted.
I can stop any time.'*

Sarah threw away the now-empty tin she had been sniffing, and angrily turned to me.

'Leave me alone, can't you? Its none of your business, anyway.'

I looked at the cross face of the ten-year-old, and wondered if her mother had guessed that the spots and rash around her mouth were not signs of premature adolescence but of the habit she insisted was not an addiction.

Her parents were struggling to make ends meet and sometimes went without meals in order to try to feed the children regularly. Sarah, who was the eldest, felt too much was expected of her. Sniffing was one way she tried to assert her own individuality in a world which, she had told me once in graphic and colourful language, did not seem to care much for her welfare. It seemed an ironic paradox that she both yearned to be allowed to be a young girl, and yet chose to indulge in such a very dangerous adult activity.

Addiction to a huge variety of stimulants runs through every level of our society. There seem to be so many Sarahs of all ages, living in quiet desperation, who take drugs to dull lives that seem to have become meaningless, purposeless or valueless.

What is this desperation to escape? And from what? Is life really so awful for so many?

What is it that is lacking from people's lives that drives so many, and such a wide variety, to seek escape from reality: and is it now so woven into the fabric of our society that we will have to accept it as a new form of reality?

Why is the prospect of facing each day with our ordinary selves, unstimulated by drugs of one sort or another, so very difficult for so many of us? Is it an indictment on society more than on the individual: and who should take the blame?

The questions come thick and fast as soon as you start to think about the subject.

When I think of Sarah and her friends, I know that the environment in which they have to grow is not one that encourages flourishing. Poor housing, high unemployment, high crime, and a general lack of hope characterise the area. The majority of individuals there though, despite their surroundings, do amazing things with very little and manage to live creative and good lives – which says more for their ingenuity, strength of spirit, and doggedness of character than for the society which allows huge inequalities of housing and opportunity to be such an integral part of our communities.

And yet, reliance on stimulants of one sort or another is also rife in areas of good housing, employment and opportunity.

In areas such as Sarah's, personal expectation is too often forced downward in order to bear with so much that is so difficult, and yet the awareness and anger of the injustice of it all still lies under the surface. The opposite is too often true in affluent areas, where expectation by self and by others is raised ever higher, thus causing its own type of stress.

What a temptation, then, to turn to tranquillisers, drink, drugs and so on, to give a sense of temporary wellbeing and relief.

When we have taken account of society's guilt and shortcomings, which are great, I do wonder whether there does not have to come a time in our lives when we have to take responsibility for what we do, and what we are. Instead of looking for the quick fix, the quick buzz, to try to take back the control and to be looking for something deeper and longer-lasting; to be putting back the meaning and value into our lives in one way or another.

Victor Frankl is a psychologist who spent most of the

Second World War in concentration camps. He counselled many looking for meaning in that horror and, in doing so, he discovered something very important; it was those who found some meaning, some purpose for living even in that situation, who had a greatly increased chance of survival.

> The secret and the purpose of living is to grow deeper
> and deeper in your response;
> to change deliberately in the light of
> a new set of circumstances,
> in order that you may go out and live
> and work in this new life. (29)

I wonder, would his hard-won philosophy be useful today for those who feel the need to turn to drugs of some sort or another in order to put some meaning, some purpose, back into life?

He also said:

> A faulty upbringing exonerates nobody:
> it has to be surmounted by conscious effort. (30)

Challenging words. For Victor Frankl is saying that there has to come a time when we cannot continue to blame our circumstances, our past, our parents, and so on, for what is wrong in our lives, if we are to live in a truly triumphant way.

> Once,
> a wounded man stumbled, fell
> and knew the depths of despair,
> the wells of loneliness.
> He allowed this to happen to himself
> in order to show the rest of humankind
> that he understood what it was
> to drink such dregs.
>
> His name is Jesus.

Jesus,
I bring before you
my broken hopes,
my dreams that have died,
the disillusionment and the
reality gone so sour
that life tastes foully curdled.

I bring before you
and lay at the foot
of your Cross
all that traps and
holds and imprisons:
the despair,
the darkness,
the pills,
potions,
needles
that fix me to
my particular tree.

Take them,
take this sense of
hollow meaninglessness,
take them all.
Transform them,
and help me to see
responding to the life
I've been given
means taking
responsibility
for my life:
that I am a
co-worker with you
in my destiny.
Amen.

Talents

'Listen!' said Hildegard, with a finger to her lips.

'There was once a king sitting on his throne.
'Around him stood great and wonderfully beautiful columns ornamented with ivory, bearing the banners of the king with great honour.
'Then it pleased the king to raise a small feather from the ground, and he commanded it to fly.
'The feather flew, not because of anything in itself, but because the air bore it along.

'Thus am I, a feather on the Breath of God.' (31)

In 1106, whilst she was still a small child, Hildegard was placed in the care of a community of nuns. When she was 43 years of age, and now Abbess of her Community, she saw tongues of flame descend from the heavens and settle upon her.

From then on, her life brimmed over with a passionate creativity.

She wrote many books on subjects ranging from medicine and natural history, to poetry, plays and music. She became the most celebrated woman of her age, renowned as a visionary, naturalist, playwright, poetess and composer.

She was internationally acclaimed, and involved herself in diplomacy and politics. Her advice and friendship were sought and prized by emperors and kings, abbots and abbesses, archbishops and popes; with all of whom she corresponded regularly.

Hildegard of Bingen opened herself to the creative power of God, which then flowed richly through her, and out into the world.

She danced to the tune of the Spirit.

She is just one, wonderful, example of the enduring and eternal nature of the Spirit breathed into humankind by the Breath of God, releasing who-knows-what gifts to be used to his greater glory.

> When Pentecost day came round, they had all met together,
>   when suddenly there came from heaven a sound
>   as of a violent wind
>   which filled the entire house in which they were sitting;
>   and there appeared to them tongues as of fire;
> these separated and came to rest on the head of each of them.
>
>   They were all filled with the Holy Spirit . . .
>   (Acts 2:1-4a.)

Down the centuries, from then to now, she has continued to inspire and guide countless numbers of people through her writings and through her music.

In 1994, 900 years after her birth, a CD of her music, entitled 'A Feather on the Breath of God', became the Classical CD of the Year.

Hildegard used her gifts to bless others. God does not give us gifts to hide them away, but to flower in another's need – as the Parable of the Talents reminds us. (Matthew 25:14f.)

One of the most original and most precious gifts I have ever received was given to me by my then nine-year-old daughter who, on Christmas morning, bade me to sit down, close my eyes, and listen – and everyone else to be quiet.

After a moment or two, the hush was broken by the sound of her flute.

It was my favourite carol. She had been rehearsing it secretly for weeks, and now she played it beautifully, the sweet clear notes singing out their praise:

> Silent night, holy night.
> Son of God, love's pure light
> radiant beams from thy holy face,
> with the dawn of redeeming grace:
> Jesus, Lord at thy birth. (32)

Joseph Mohr was the writer of 'Silent Night', which has been one of the most beloved of all carols. I wonder, when he wrote it, did he have a sense he was writing something very special, that he was penning something that would bless many generations of people?

Did Hildegard too have a sense, through those hidden years leading up to her profound mystical experience and the gifting that was the result, that she was moving towards some particular destination, some particular task, she knew not what but would know it when it came? Or, perhaps, had she prayed, passionately and persistently, for the very things that she was finally given?

Jesus urges us to pray in faith and earnestly, without ceasing, for those things for which we most long.

On one occasion, he told his disciples a Parable about the Persistent Widow as an illustration of the need to pray continually and never to lose heart (Luke 18:1-8).

We need to be careful, though, that we really do want what we pray for.

Mother Julian of Norwich, the famous medieval mystic, prayed most passionately that she might be privileged to share in the suffering and death of her Lord. Her prayer was answered. In her writings, *Revelations of Divine Love*, she records graphically the vision she was given of the full horror of such a violent and terrible death.

'Ask!'

'I ask that you
will gift me with the ability
to glorify you
in word and line:
that I shall be able
to speak,
to write,
to draw
the ache in my heart
for the beauty of
your Creation
and of my love
for you.'

Silence.

I become absorbed
once more
in just looking.

Then –

a
still
small
voice:

'Your prayer
shall be
answered.'

CAUGHT AND HELD

God
held out the gift.

'I
offer this
to you',
he said.

'But you must
reach out and
take it.

'It's a knock-down
put-it-together-yourself
kind of kit:
the pieces are all there –

'but you
are the glue.'

I am reminding you now
to fan into a flame the gift
God has given you.
(2 Timothy 1:6)

Bad Memories

> Can you not minister to a mind diseased,
> pluck from the memory a rooted sorrow,
> raze out the written troubles of the brain? (33)

> I remember, oh yes I remember,
> the house where I was born . . .

. . . It had an enormous weeping willow tree in the back garden, higher than the house. My father had hung a ship's rope from one of the upper branches, so its swing was tremendous and at the end there was a huge knot for a seat. One of our favourite games was to swing as far and as high as we could, and then jump off seeing who could get the furthest.

The tree was also our den – a hiding place deep in the branches and foliage, and our look-out post. One day when I was four years of age, my older brothers pushed and pulled me to the top of the tree because they thought I would enjoy the view, but then could not get me down again, and so my mother had to climb up and retrieve me. She was into fresh air in a big way and, when we had the usual childhood ailments and if it was summer and warm, she would wrap us up and put us on a bed under the tree during the day. The great sweeping fronds hung down and around like a protective curtain.

When we weren't swinging or hiding, we were running free through the fields and woods, or fishing and making dams in the stream, near our home. But that weeping willow tree has always remained for me the central symbol of my early childhood freedom.

When I was eight we moved to a much larger house. As I watched the removal men lugging in the furniture and boxes a foreboding, the intensity of which I can remember to this day, suddenly came over me. I knew with the piercingly clear vision of a child that from now on it would all be different: that that previous infinitely precious time was over. And I felt a great, seemingly unbearable, well of grief surge up from deep within me for what had gone from my life. It was as if a switch had been thrown. The ability to be aware of such a truth changed me that day from a child to a little adult, and from innocence to worldly wise.

> Tears from the depths of some divine despair rise . . .
> in thinking of the days that are 'no more'. (34)

Was I being prepared to be strong enough to bear what was to happen a few years later: when I was fifteen years old and my father died suddenly and, exactly a year after that, when the young man I wanted one day to marry was killed, aged nineteen years of age? Close on the footsteps of these came more dark times.

All the above events, the good and the bad, are indelibly imprinted on my memory along with, of course, many, many others all woven finely together into the tapestry marked 'childhood'. Also, of course, the threads are not all tidily contained under that label and many have escaped to trail their many-coloured strands through my adult years; some to good effect and some to the opposite.

It is strange how the good times strengthen you for the bad. I am sure that those early golden days (which probably in reality contained a number of rainy ones as well, only I don't remember them) laid seeds which were later to be harvested in all sorts of ways. And then, when I was eight, when he thought I was ready, God took my hand and gently but firmly led me on to the next stage of my development so that I would be prepared for what was to come.

For this is how I think God intervenes in our, and his, world: not by altering events so much as by altering us, and changing us, and moving us on. By calling to us and by being there when we call on him – although his answer may not appear in the shape or form or way in which we expect, or even hope, at the time.

Compared to the terrible memories some have to bear, mine pale into insignificance. And I was so fortunate to have had those early years on which to draw when I needed them. For so many others this is not so; and for many more the bad memories haunt them to the degree that they prevent them living in the now. What to do in such situations?

A lot of people have been helped by walking through the events in their imagination with Jesus as their close companion. They picture his healing presence in the midst of that which is causing so much pain, remembering the pain he himself bore on the cross and which links him so intimately to our suffering.

I, too, have found it very helpful. In my experience, each time you try it, more healing seems to take place. It is as though Jesus is progressively lifting more of the pain from my shoulders onto his, and freeing me up to be more fully in the present.

Part of the particular pain of bad memories can be the sense of God's absence at that time; that, at the time of your greatest need, he did not seem to be there for you.

Have you ever tried to draw your faith journey? It is when you take a sheet of paper and mark on it an undulating line to represent the main downs and ups in your life from birth to the present. Then mark in where you are aware now, even if you weren't then, of God's presence in the events of your life. Return to it several times, and you will probably find that there are more and more events you want to mark with God's presence.

It can be a steep learning curve as to the goodness of God and his continuous activity in our lives: unseen, unfelt, and sometimes seemingly very absent maybe but, nevertheless, in reality always present and active.

Memories can hold you back in the past, freezing you into inability to function fully in the present, as happened with Lot's wife:

> When dawn broke the angels urged Lot and his family,
> 'Flee for your life. Do not look behind you . . .'
> But Lot's wife did look back,
> and was turned into a pillar of salt.
> (Genesis 19:15f)

Or they can be a resource, a learning experience, a strength. And that is what prophecy really is: using the experiences of the past to inform the present.

Our memory is the record of our history and it is important for our peace of mind and for our mental health that we try to remember truly. It can be tempting to recall only the bad things from our past if we are wanting to justify what we see as failure in the present, for we can then blame these events and hook our failures on to them.

It is important too, that we do not try to recreate the past in order to bring it inappropriately into the present, for this does not usually work – as I found out:

Some years ago, I decided to grow a weeping willow tree just like the one from my earliest childhood. I bought a young sapling and trained the branches down in the way friends with similar trees had told me I should. But I was puzzled at my sapling's reluctance to 'weep'.

Then, one day, a friend who had not visited for a while saw my tree and became very excited. 'You've got one of those!' she exclaimed. 'They're really quite rare.'

'Weeping willow trees aren't rare', I said.

'That's not a *weeping* willow. It's the opposite: a *corkscrew* willow. Its branches twist upwards, not hang down.' She went over, and released the strings and pegs that were holding the branches down, and they sprang up towards the sky as if rejoicing in their newfound freedom. 'See', she said. 'Isn't it beautiful?'

She was right. I looked at the delicately curling and twisting branches and leaves, and realised how I had been so caught up in recreating the past, that I had not seen what was really before my eyes. It really is a most beautiful tree, my corkscrew willow, and has given me so much pleasure ever since – now that I value it for what it truly is and not for what I thought I wanted it to be.

As it matured, long delicate fronds also hung down and trailed to the ground creating a canopy of cool and shade. It is as if, having allowed it to be what it was always intended to be, it has been released to be more for me as well.

> From the downcast sorrow of
> the weeping willow,
> to the upturned joy of the
> branches and leaves
> spiralling, corkscrewing their
> way heavenward –
> God sees the
> beauty and potential
> of them both.

CAUGHT AND HELD

Memories,
Lord,
lifting from the very
deepest part of me and
bringing the past
into today.
Painful, anguished, bitter
sweet or breathcatchingly
beautiful, they are some of
the woven fine fabric
shaping me.

Thank you for the good,
Lord, and help me
not to drown in the bad.
Take my hand and
walk with me down that rockstrewn lane,
breathing, touching,
healing, redeeming
the hurt, the sadness, the pain.

Help me to remember they
are not my whole story;
that I am so very much more.
The past has passed,
the future is yet to be born.
So, Lord,
past, present, future, I place
in your hands.
Take it, shape it, and make of it
what you will.

Amen.

Communication

> Honey bees have a sophisticated waggle dance
> which points other bees towards
> the nearest flowers.

> 'What is the use of a book',
> thought Alice,
> 'without pictures or conversations?' (35)

> Let your conversation be always
> full of grace,
> seasoned with salt . . .
> (Colossians 4:6)

Rockets to the moon and beyond, messages bounced off satellites, Internet and E-mail, fax machines and telephones and soon, we are promised, we will be able to use our computers as video-phone screens.

No longer then will we be able to hide behind the anonymity of voice-only communication: each phone will require a mirror to be hung beside it so that we can check our appearance before we answer. And, of course, we will need a shelf as well on which to place the wherewithal to make any hasty adjustments.

All a far cry from a century ago when even the telephone was still a most basic instrument.

Then, parents who waved their children off to the New World did not expect ever to see them again. Now they can have near-instant communication with offspring, wherever they are, and in a variety of ways.

And yet all this super-sophistication has not replaced in

the slightest our need for the simple first-hand encounter and contact, the meeting of eye or hand, the smile, the quiet word.

As humans we are born into community, and we need each other. It is a well-known fact that tiny babies who are not touched and talked to regularly soon begin to pine away. Communication is essential to their survival: they are literally touched and talked into life; just as God touched and talked Creation into life.

I wonder, was it that first Touch, those first Words, which created in us such a longing, such a desire, for communication with one other? Only when totally isolated from it do we, perhaps, *truly* value it?

I shall never forget how I felt when a friend shared with me a dream she had. It was, she said, one of those dreams which are so realistic that for some time after you wake you are unsure whether you are still in the dream; unsure of what is the reality. I tell it to you now as she told it to me.

'It was a post-nuclear-bomb world, barren and devastated.

'A great Arctic waste stretched in every direction as far as the eye could see, and a freezing wind blew continually.

'At first I thought I was alone in this desolate wasteland.

'Then I saw some other people and, with a glad cry, I reached out to them. Or, rather, I tried to. The reality was that the glad cry was only within myself. I could make no outer sound and, however hard I struggled, my arms, my whole body, seemed paralysed.

'As I gazed longingly at these people, who seemed to increase in number by the second, I realised that they too were struggling to reach out to me and to each other, but with no more success than I.

'As the timeless-time went by, I realised something else: the reason for our inability to move was a transparent film which covered each of us like a cocoon, immobilising each person and totally isolating her or him. Each of us could see,

but would never be able to communicate, with anyone else.
'We were all locked in a nightmare of non-communication.'

Fortunately, it was a nightmare from which she awoke, but the deep implication of the picture she drew has stayed with me ever since: of our need for one another. In our fiercely individualistic world of today, I wonder, are we in danger of forgetting that?

Non-communication, though, is a world apart from non-verbal communication when there is not a need for words, and where people touch at a deep level beyond speech. In *Far From the Madding Crowd*, Gabriel Oak refers to such times in his beautiful and romantic proposal of marriage to Bathsheba:

> 'And home by the fire
> whenever you look up
> there I shall be –
> and whenever I look up,
> there will be you.' (36)

How different from my friend's dream.

Most dreams, so the psychologists tell us, are like stories and are the mind's attempts to match and to link together all sorts of recent and past events, experiences, thoughts and feelings; scanning, sorting and rearranging them in order to make sense of them.

Most dreams also are ephemeral, and trying to remember them is like trying to catch hold of mist, but some are so vivid that there is no problem of recall. As these can often contain some important information from the subconscious they are worth reflecting upon to see what is being communicated.

They are messages to yourself from deep within yourself;

maybe, even, messages from the God who resides at the deepest part of ourselves and who is in constant loving communication and dialogue with each of us, even when we are unaware of it.

'Your heart is my hermitage',

said Thomas Merton, Cistercian monk and hermit. His words illustrate perfectly how closely intertwined we are with one another, and therefore how concerned we should be for one another's welfare.

The words could be those of God, describing how intimately he is intertwined with each one of us.

Lord,
from the most sophisticated
interplanetary technology to the
face-to-face dialogue
of friends, and
the non-verbal intimacy
of lovers where
words are superfluous
and communication is
by silence;
each reaches out to
the other.

Humanity and Nature –
all of your creation
in constant communication.

I picture your Cross –
stretching from
heaven and planted on Earth,
down whose shaft
poured the love of
the Father, mingling with your own,
to bring new life
to humanity.

Arms held open –
wide open
in an anguish of
loving communication:
'How much do you love me?'
I asked.
'This much', you said, and
opened wide your arms
and died.

STRESS

In a world of change
Instead of struggling to swim,
We must learn to breathe water. (37)

'Do you have a feeling of tightness in your chest?
Are you tired/very tired/exhausted all the time,
yet cannot sleep properly when you do eventually get to bed?
Do you feel you are running in order to stand still? . . .'

trumpeted the leaflet on stress, making me feel quite stressful just reading it.

In our fast-moving and stress-filled world, Sisyphus – he was sentenced to spend eternity pushing that boulder up that hill; his terrible fate being that whenever it was almost at the top it rolled back down to the bottom again – is certainly a person with whom very many people could identify.

It is universally acknowledged – as Jane Austen might have said – that a certain amount of stress is essential: without it we would topple over in a heap on the floor.

It can also give us a buzz, turning mundane days into ones with a sense of excitement as we hurtle from one commitment to another, and a feeling of living life to the full.

Yet, if we have reached the stage of a good friend of mine, who lives life in the fast lane both at work and at leisure – and who admitted recently, 'I daren't stop' – is it not time to take back the control? Then to place it in the hands of the one who, if we would only dare to trust, will take the stress – the negative energy – and transform it into a positive and creative force, based on a sense of peace and wholeness, rather than on fragmentation and tension.

Come to me, all you who labour and are overburdened,
and I will give you rest.
(Matthew 11:28)

With these words, Jesus invites us to cast our cares, our stress and distress, on to him, and assures us that we should not be afraid, should not feel out of control – for his strength, his love, are with us always and will sustain us.

However, easier said than done for most of us!

What should people like my 'daren't stop' friend do in order to respond to such an invitation?

How can he, and all the others, slow down enough to hand over the control in the first place?

It is difficult, if not impossible, to still the mind if your body is tightly coiled and muscles tensed. If we are to relax our minds, we have first to learn to relax our bodies as well.

Below are some relaxation techniques which I, and many others, have found very helpful. Do try them. They won't take long, and they really do make a difference: as my 'daren't stop' friend found out when eventually I managed to persuade him to try it. Recently, he reluctantly admitted they had made an amazing difference to him as now he *chooses* when, and when not, to relax.

Find a quiet space, a still place, and a comfortable firm chair. Get into a relaxed position, but not slouching, with uncrossed legs, feet on the floor, and with unclasped hands resting on your lap.

Close your eyes, and spend a few moments concentrating on getting your breathing even and gentle. As you exhale, think the words, 'relax, let go'.

Then relax the whole of your body by concentrating on it, bit by bit. Start at the top of your head, and work down, becoming aware of each part. Any part that feels particularly tense, imagine as a coiled spring, or a block of ice, or a rope tied in a knot; then imagine that tense object uncoiling, melting, relaxing, loosening.

Return to concentrating on your breathing; now breathing in 'Jesus', and breathing out 'me'.

Try not to think of any noises you hear as distractions, but draw them in to your quiet time, thereby transforming them. Or else, picture small white clouds passing by and drop the distractions, whether they be noises or thoughts, onto the clouds and watch them float out of sight.

If you spend just a few minutes each day practising this, soon you will find that, if necessity requires, for example at work, you are able to 'short-circuit' the preparation time and, in a few moments, diffuse the stress which is building up.

>
> My head, my life, is spinning,
> Lord.
> So many demands upon
> me, my time, my energy.
> Multi-directional pulls yanking
> me that way and this,
> winding me up to a
> rack-stretched-stress-level until I
> feel my nerves will
> crack with the strain.
> Rushing headlong through my life
> I accomplish less and
> less and less
> the harder
> I
> try.

Now I come to think of it,
Lord,
there's an inverse proportion between
my stressed-out effort and
your controlled way of
working and
walking;
between my speed and
your measured step;
between my achievement
and yours.

Where are your footprints,
Lord?
Unwind me,
slow me down,
that I may fall into
step behind you
and walk
beside
you —
at your pace,
not mine.

Amen.

The Lord is my Pace-setter;
I shall not rush.
He makes me stop and rest for quiet intervals.
He provides me with images of stillness,
which restore my serenity.
He leads me in ways of efficiency, through calmness of mind;
and his guidance is peace.
Even though I have a great many things
to accomplish each day,
I will not fret, for his presence is here;
his timelessness, his all-importance,
will keep me in balance.
He prepares refreshment and renewal
in the midst of my activity,
by anointing my mind with the oils of his tranquillity.
My cup of joyous energy overflows.
Truly harmony and effectiveness shall be
the fruits of my hours.
For I shall walk in the pace of my Lord,
and dwell in his house for ever. (38)

Words ... Art ... Music

*There is a close link from birth for us
between words and music and art,
and our inmost self.*

'Now I know there is a God in heaven',
said Albert Einstein on hearing the child prodigy
Yehudi Menuhin playing the violin.

Prose, poetry, sculpture, painting and music have all been ways in which humankind has sought to express its deepest feelings.

Cave-paintings, many thousand years old, have been discovered in widely diverse geographical areas.

Ancient civilisations indicated status and power by the intricacy of carving on pottery, jewellery and other possessions. The amazingly delicate and beautiful artwork astounding even modern artists, with modern tools at their disposal, as to its execution and sophistication.

Even before writing became the universal means of communication, the community's common experience was told from generation to generation in story form. The storytellers were much respected people, with phenomenal memories.

And music – which can bring to birth the deepest part of ourselves, articulating that which we have not yet fully enough understood in order to put into words.

When my mother was three months pregnant with me, and my father was very ill in a London hospital, she went to hear Fritz Kreisler, the great violinist, at the Albert Hall.

The music flowed over her and through her, soothing her distressed heart and mind, and reviving her sense of hope. She sat through the matinee, and then the evening performance, profoundly aware of how life-giving this music was being for her, and how needed.

It was during the second performance that she felt me kick for the first time; not just once, but rhythmically, in time to the music.

Ever since I can remember, the violin has been the supreme instrument for me. It seems to speak to the very deepest parts of my being. Certain violin pieces represent for me the profoundest feelings, and my family know when I play them that I am either very happy or very sad.

I did not know the story of my mother's visit to that concert until I was in my teens, and so it cannot be that the knowledge of it influenced my empathy with violin music. However, when I did finally hear it, I knew it as a moment of the deepest truth.

In a very real way I had been played into life, brought to life, the day of that concert. The music had not only been life-giving to my mother, but to me also.

One theory about the basic building blocks of the universe is that they are not particles but wave-forms which have been given the name superstrings. This is both a very ancient, and a very modern, idea.

This theory holds that billions upon billions of unseen strings pervade the universe, and their different frequencies give rise to all the matter and energy in creation. Certain vibrations also turn into time and space. In this theory, then, primordial sound is the basic building block.

In the beginning, God created heaven and earth. God said . . .
(Genesis 1:1, 3a)

And so Creation was played, and spoken, into existence. Perhaps this is the reason why there is such a close link from birth for us humans between words and music. Janáček, it is said, used to collect sentences, compose music around them, and then throw away the words.

God created order and meaning out of chaos. As humans we also need to make sense, and create patterns and order, out of the huge variety of information we receive. When we do perceive a pattern it gives us, the psychologists say, great satisfaction, and excites our curiosity to continue the investigation further. Just so with music. A pleasing melody satisfies our need for harmony. The mixture of dissonance and harmony in a piece also reflects our understanding of the way life is.

Memory, emotion and music seem to be rooted in the very anatomy of our brains, and in the very depths of our hearts. Music finds echoes in these deepest parts of us, drawing together many fragments of experiences, memories, feelings and making sense of them, putting us in touch with these aspects and making us feel whole again.

> He has put a new song in my mouth,
> a hymn of praise to our God.
> Many will see and fear
> and put their trust in the Lord.
> (Psalm 40:3)

Words and music combined, in praise of the Lord. Add in art, and there can be few more holistic experiences.

An unforgettable experience for me was when I heard a recording of Haydn's 'Creation' whilst glorious paintings and camera shots of appropriate scenes were played across a screen. The combination of sight and sound were an absolute feast and delight.

There seems at times to be a mysterious interconnection of creativity between those seeking to reach into new areas of expression from very different disciplines. It is said that at just the same time as the great painter Turner was reaching his sublime heights in the painting of light, a scientist discovered the exact speed of light.

When words fail us, we can often turn to painting or drawing to express our deepest feelings. Psychologists regularly get their patients to draw out their inmost distress and conflicts. And you have only to see the absolute delight of little children let loose with paints to realise how at one with the paints they feel.

One of my favourite photographs is of my daughter one summer, then aged three years, painting in the garden. She is wearing only a pair of shorts and a sunhat, and there is not only paint all over the paper on the easel, but all over her as well. Paper-painting, body-painting, there was no demarcation for her; all was one. The rapt and faraway expression on her face indicates how totally absorbed she is in the whole activity.

On several occasions Jesus bent down and drew or wrote in the sand. Each time it was at a moment of significance. Was he just playing for time whilst he decided what it was he wanted to say – or was there a deeper meaning?

> The scribes and Pharisees brought a woman caught
> in the act of adultery before Jesus,
> and asked him what he had to say on the matter.
> They asked him this as a test, looking for an accusation
> to use against him.
> But Jesus bent down and started writing on the ground
> with his finger.
> As they persisted with their question,
> he straightened up and said,
> Let the one among you who is guiltless be the first
> to throw a stone at her.
> Then he bent down and continued writing on the ground.
> (John 8:3f)

John's Gospel is not renowned for superfluous, insignificant detail. Why would he have put this story in if it had no meaning? For two thousand years people have argued why.

The Gospel of John is just one part of that book of so many parts: the Bible – ultimate example of wonderful writing, and source of inspiration to humankind in every aspect of its civilisation.

> Great and wide as the world,
> rooted in the depths of creation
> and soaring up to the blue mysteries of heaven . . .
> sunset and sunrise,
> denial and fulfilment,
> birth and death,
> the whole drama of humanity –
> all is found in this book. (39)

> Thank you,
> Lord,
> for the joys of poetry and prose,
> sculpture, painting
> and music;
>
> for prefiguring our human efforts
> in the wonders of your effortless
> creation;
>
> for shaping and painting,
> speaking and playing
> this glorious rainbow world
> into existence.
>
> You
> Lord
> are the
> Supreme
> Artist.
>
> Amen.

SHADOW AND LIGHT

Suffering

'Why!?'

The anguished cry of the 18-year-old with multiple problems
could only be received in silence.
The one word held a world of suffering within it.
Any immediate answer would have seemed trite
and a denial of his suffering.

His prayers seemed to have fallen on deaf ears,
as far as he was concerned.

So – why *does* God seem to heal some and not others?
This vexed question has perplexed and preoccupied humankind through the ages.
If it is down to the quality or the quantity of prayer offered up by the sufferer, or on their behalf, does that not also seem unfair? What about those who do not know how to pray, or who have no one to pray for them?
It cannot be that God has preferences, for the Bible often tells us that he has no favourites and that all are equal in the sight of God:
'Then Peter began to speak:
"I now realise how true it is that God does not show
favouritism . . ."'
(Acts 10:34)

Suffering can be like water, seeping into every area of life, every fibre of one's body, overwhelming every other feeling, and giving a sense of powerlessness and helplessness that there is nothing the sufferer can do to alleviate the suffering.
There is a strand of Christian thought which teaches

suffering is, in itself and for its own sake, enobling and purifying; as if, somehow, pain – whether psychological, physical or social – is intrinsically good. However, that seems to me to be very like the sort of consolation which used often to be fed to slaves to make them content with their lot: those who suffer in this world are assured of better things in the world to come.

By this reckoning it could be argued the rich man was doing the poor man Lazarus a favour by letting him starve to death at his gate (Luke 16:19f).

Suffering is understood by many more as a test sent by God, which we are required to pass – despite the fact the Bible again and again seeks to dispel this notion and, rather, presents suffering as a product of human selfishness and misuse of the original intention of God's creation catching up guilty and innocent alike.

If we project suffering outwards onto God we can give a kind of meaning to something that might otherwise feel so meaningless. However, it can also absolve the rest of us from any serious attempt to change the situations and the structures that cause suffering.

It seems to me that if God the Father also suffers, not 'just' through Christ but intrinsically in himself, then would not suffering be bound to be finely woven into the very fabric of our lives, too?

If suffering is part of God's very nature then, when we suffer, we must be linked with that part of God: just as when we love we must be linked to the love of God.

If to be able to feel anger or delight, sadness or joy, helps to define our humanity then would not suffering also be integral to our human condition?

All of this, though, still does not solve the mystery of suffering nor answer the questions of whether our suffering has a redemptive purpose for each of us, or whether it is God's will we suffer.

There is a paradox here: suffering can surely only be a product of our fallen world – and yet it was through the suffering Christ our fallen world is redeemed.

Could it possibly be then, I wonder, that some of the answer lies in the whole concept of freedom?

God loves us enough to give us freedom to make choices. So, then, should we not also do the same for him?

By this reckoning he is not an arbitrary God, a trigger-happy God who fires off rounds of suffering indiscriminately at a helpless humankind, but a God who has the freedom to heal as he chooses and, in his wisdom, as he sees fit.

Have we just described one big circle, arriving back at precisely the same point from which we set out, and still asking the same question:

Why?

No, I don't think so.

For, as we struggle to understand a little more these great mysteries of life and of living, we move up and down the twists and turns of the spiral of discernment, but never arrive back at the same point from which we started – although it may, at times, feel that way.

Each question, each twist and turn, takes us a little deeper into the mystery and makes us wiser than we were before.

Alan Ecclestone was a fiery, strong-speaking, often controversial Anglican priest, who chose to spend many years of his active ministry in parishes in the Inner City of his beloved Sheffield.

One day, a few years before he died, he said to me:

> 'You should take all the statements,
> the deep imponderables, of life
> and turn them into questions.
> Promise me you will never stop asking questions.'

'Dearest Father,
I'm puzzled
and confused:
your so-beautiful world
created with infinite
imagination and
sensitivity and
sense of humour too;
so –
how and where
on earth
did suffering slip in
like a slithering
slippery
sliding-on-its-belly
snake?
Was
it all a
terrible
mistake?'

'Darling one,
your perception
is from
down-side-up,
mine
from
up-side-down.
When you have the
wisdom of
angels,

> then
> I
> shall explain;
> when you have
> the wisdom of
> angels
> I
> shan't
> need to.'

Jesus used his suffering for the benefit of others, thereby pointing the way for us.

In our desire to remove suffering, are we trying to sanitise the world in the same way we too often try to sanitise the Cross?

'Apatheia' is a Greek word whose literal meaning is non-suffering. From it we derive our English word 'apathy': a person described as apathetic conjures up a picture of someone who is lethargic and beyond caring.

> Under the Church of the Nativity, in Bethlehem,
> in one of the bare, stark, subterranean caves
> well off the tourist trail,
> I found a crucifix hanging on the wall.
>
> The twisted and tortured limbs of the cross
> were mirrored
> in the twisted and tortured limbs
> of the man
> hanging there.
>
> Suffering seemed to scream out of the silent figure.

God become Man
who chose that agonising way
of returning to God:
through his suffering giving
infinite meaning to suffering,
and thereby
planting his cross firmly
in every place
where there is pain
of any kind.

LAUGHTER

In the laughter of children
may be heard the
song of the angels . . .

I don't know whether you have found – but I certainly have – that my own mood seems directly to affect the way the rest of the world functions.

It is as if there is a direct link or correlation.

I mean, if I am feeling grouchy and bad-tempered that is the way people seem to be back to me. If, on the other hand, I am feeling on top of the world then the world seems to smile back to me.

I wonder, is it a matter of perception? If that is the case, then how I am becomes a matter of supreme importance. If by being one way or another I can affect my surroundings so profoundly – or at least my perception of it – then I am a very powerful person indeed, and my mood matters tremendously.

I had, as they say, got out of bed on the wrong side one morning and consequently I burnt the toast, put my foot through my tights, and all the usual disasters that can pile up before 8am had done so, or so it seemed. And it had happened on a day in which I knew I would be hurrying from one commitment to the next until evening.

Things went from this not very promising beginning to much worse. Each negative encounter seemed to spill over, with greater and greater backwash, into the following ones.

Matters were not improved by the puzzled reactions of others. 'You're usually in such a good mood/such a sunny person. What's wrong?' merely served to underline the unreasonableness of the way I was, and the question pursued me through the day in different shapes and forms and with varying gentleness.

And it was not just people with whom I seemed at odds. Machines seemed to pick up the vibes: my car sounded as if it had blown a hole in the exhaust; my computer went down and lost some work (through my own fault, my arm catching the main switch as I leaned across to get something); and I had misread my diary: the meeting had begun an hour earlier than I realised, and I huffed and puffed in very late and very embarrassed.

By the time evening came, I was ready to forsake the world and become a hermit.

As I stomped back into home dreaming of a long hot soak in exotic bath oils, and an even longer drink, I heard my daughter and son laughing and laughing about something.

My daughter's laugh is of the irresistibly infectious kind and I smiled to myself, for what seemed the first time that day, as I heard it. My son observed, with characteristic frankness, how fed up I was looking, before continuing with the story he was telling.

Immediately, I was drawn deep into their conversation and what was making them laugh so much. My son's gift for self-deprecating mimicry added to the humour of it all, and soon I was laughing too, until tears ran down my face.

I told them of my day, and the recounting of it put it all into perspective, making me realise the insignificance of so much that had seemed so important – and we ended up laughing at me.

My tiredness and irritability melted away in the merriment, and a lightness of mood settled in their place. A sense of peace descended and, for the first time that day, I felt at one with myself.

As I soaked in that bath, with that drink on the side, the continuing laughter downstairs drifted up and embraced me.

My mind went back down the years to when my now-grown-up children were tiny, then returned slowly to the present. Through all that time their laughter echoed as a celebration of life turning sometimes dull days, negative days – as today – into something quite other.

There had been tears too, of course; not to have remembered those would have been a denial of the reality of life's sadnesses and sorrows and pain. But it was the life-affirming laughter that predominated in my memory.

And their laughter had infinitely sweetened my life too.

Psychologists have long been telling us that if we smile on the outside it will not be long before we are smiling on the inside as well. Apparently, we find it very difficult to live for long with the contradiction of a happy outer self and a miserable inner self. A dissonance is set up within us which has to be resolved, and we have to make a decision as to which aspect of self we are going to choose.

It is as if we have a very strong need for unity, for oneness, for order, built into the deepest part of ourselves; not just in our brains but in our hearts as well, and which keeps trying to assert itself.

I wonder, is that why puzzles of all sorts hold such a fascination for us, and why the solving of them gives us such satisfaction?

When I look around at our divided world, so in need of that which will unify it, it gives me hope and encouragement that there *is* such a drive in each one of us, for change begins with the individual.

If every individual has this deep inbuilt yearning for oneness, for cohesion, rather than fragmentation – although many might not express it that way or even consciously be aware of it – then it becomes a global yearning or experience: the collective unconscious as Jung, that greatest of psychologists, described it.

And global yearnings are what fuel change on a global scale.

So, our moods really *do* matter.

You could even say that the future of the world depends on what choice we make.

In the laughter of children
can be heard the
song of the angels;
God's
gifting to
the world.

Running like liquid gold
through the whole of Creation
is your sense of humour,
Lord,
your laughter
and merriment.

The world was born and is borne
on the wings of your joy
in all you have created.
Open wide my heart
to this
life-giving river.

May it flow
through me
and out
into
the world.

Amen

Injustice

What stronger breastplate than a heart untainted!
Thrice armed is he whose quarrel is just;
and he, though locked up in steel, is naked,
whose conscience with injustice is corrupted. (40)

Let justice flow like a river,
and righteousness like a never-failing stream . . .
says the Lord your God.
(Amos 5:24)

An Archbishop of Canterbury and a Pope both die and arrive at the Pearly Gates together. They are surprised to hear from St Peter that *everyone* has to undergo a test before they can enter heaven. 'Spell "God"', Peter tells them. They do so correctly and pass through.

A while later a woman priest arrives at the Pearly Gates, and Peter tells her she must first pass a test. She is very upset and angry. 'All my working life,' she declares, 'I've had to put up with the injustice of prejudice. I've had to do twice as well as the men to achieve the same things.' She reeled off a long list of examples. 'All right then', she sighed. 'What's the test?'

'Spell "Mephistopheles"', Peter replied.

This lighthearted story would resonate with the opposite-of-lighthearted experiences for those who have known prejudice and discrimination, whether of belief, sexism, racism, homophobia, class, and so on. The list increases as society in general becomes more and more aware of its tendency to treat its various members unequally.

Like most humorous stories which also have the ring of truth about them, it illustrates how those caught in the web of injustice often have this sense that it is never-ending: that it just goes on and on and on, if not in one form then in another.

There is so much pain and bewilderment, felt by so many sections of society on a global as well as more local levels, of people who know the evil of discrimination of one sort or another in their lives.

Injustice comes in so many forms, and has so many disguises, that I wonder if there is a person on earth who has not practised it, consciously or unconsciously, at some time or another. It is something of which we are all guilty. Maybe, when we are realistic and honest enough to see it, and admit it, then real change, beginning with the individual, will happen.

Responding to prolonged discussion in the newspapers about what was the root cause of society's ills, G. K. Chesterton wrote to the editor:

'Dear Sir, I am, Yours sincerely.'

Another story about heaven. However, this one is different and it illustrates how narrowminded self-righteousness can masquerade as the strictest justice but can, in fact, be supremely unjust. It is only when and where justice is tempered with love, compassion and generosity that we begin to understand, just a little, how the whole subject of justice may be perceived by God.

> God walked into heaven one day and found, to his surprise, that everyone was there. Not a single soul had been sent to hell. This disturbed him, for did he not owe it to himself to be just? And what was hell created for anyway, if the place was not going to be used?

So he said to the Angel Gabriel, 'Summon everyone before my throne and read the Ten Commandments.'

Everyone was summoned. Gabriel read the first of the Commandments. Then God said, 'All those who have sinned against this Commandment will take themselves off to hell immediately.' A number of people detached themselves from the crowd and went off sadly to hell.

A similar thing was done after the second Commandment was read . . . and the third . . . and the fourth . . . and the fifth . . . By now the population of heaven had decreased considerably. After the sixth Commandment was read, everyone had gone to hell except one person.

God looked up and said to Gabriel, 'Is this the only person left in heaven?'

'Yes,' said Gabriel.

'Well,' said God, 'it's rather lonesome here, isn't it? Tell them all to come back!' (41)

It is heartening that each generation produces giants in the struggle for justice who act as beacons of hope, and as great examplers and inspirers to the rest of us. This is particularly so if their struggle is articulated by non-violence.

Half a century ago, one such giant was Gandhi who wrote:

> 'To refuse to fight against injustice
> is to surrender your humanity.
> To fight it with the weapons of war
> is to enter your humanity.
> To fight it with the weapons of God
> is to enter your divinity.'

Then it was Martin Luther King Junior, who spoke in the most powerful and moving words of his dreams for a fair and just world where there would be no more racism.

Today, we have Nelson Mandela, who said, on the final day of his triumphant visit to London on July 12, 1996 from the balcony of South Africa House, to the many thousands gathered to see and to hear him:

'One of the striking features of modern times is the
number of men and women from all over the globe,
in all continents, who fight oppression of human rights.
These men and women have chosen the entire world
as a battlefield for their operations, as a theatre for all
their efforts. Many communities in the world now
have been able to solve their problems because of the efforts
of those men and women who have vision,
who have courage to stand for the truth and
who are prepared to suffer for it.'

One such person was Veronica Guerin, a journalist who was uncompromising in her determination to uncover the truth. Armed only with her pen, she set out to expose drug dealing rings and other criminal activities which threatened the Irish society in which she lived, regardless of the cost to herself. This eventually meant at the cost of her life, when she was gunned down on June 26, 1996, aged 33 years.

All of these people remind us that keeping silence in the face of injustice is a cop-out of our individual human responsibility to create a better, more equitable world for everyone.

As Ecclesiasticus counselled us, there is a time for silence and a time to speak. And Jesus gave us an actual example in his own life when he constantly spoke out against all that oppressed people. The only time he fell silent was in his last days, in the presence of those who were to be responsible for his death, and then his silence shouted out his innocence.

Not to take part in an injustice is to fight against it – whether it is refusing to join in gossip, speaking out in defence of another, or by standing alongside those who are suffering the injustice in whatever way seems appropriate.

Why, Lord,
why should
they treat me so harshly?
The colour of my skin –
I don't fit in to
their preconceived
notion of what
is correct.

Why, Lord, why
should they treat me so cruelly?
My accent's not right
– they say –
I'm from the wrong side
of the tracks,
I am not one
of them.

Why, Lord, why should
they treat me so badly?
It's not my fault my
dad is in jail and Mum
told me she couldn't afford
me any more.
I'm jobless, homeless, the
lowest of
the low.

Why,
Lord,
why can't they
be like
you?

You
would have
treated
me
right.

God –
may justice flow
like water
into every crack,
every seam of life
like a never-ending
river,
a raging torrent
sweeping
all before it
of prejudice,
discrimination,
narrow-minded self-righteousness
which masquerades
and disguises
and parodies
that glorious fairness
of the
Father –
help me,
help each one of us,
to play our part
to ensure justice
rolls on to
eternity like
a river, and
true righteousness
like a
never-failing
stream.

Amen.

Beauty

> A thing of beauty is a joy forever;
> it's loveliness increases; it will never
> pass away into nothingness. (42)

'Beauty lies in the eye of the beholder.'

This rather tired cliché was given new life for me on a family picnic once, when my now-grown-up children were little.

A large and very evil-looking insect had landed on my daughter's shoulder and, knowing her great dislike of any such thing, I hastily knocked it off.

'Don't do that!' exclaimed my then-five-year-old son with great indignation.

Thinking I had inadvertently flicked it on to him, I began to apologise.

'You might have hurt it – you hit it in its face', my son interrupted crossly. Kneeling on the ground he gazed in wonder at the stunned insect. 'Look – isn't she beautiful. All those *colours*. Oh Mum, don't you think she's *beautiful?*'

Kneeling beside him, I looked with some distaste at the large, rather squashed and very ugly insect. But, as my son continued to exclaim and to point out her, erstwhile hidden to me, charms I began to see her in a new light. He was right; she *was* fascinating. Whilst I could not quite stretch to his level of appreciation and call her beautiful, seeing her through his eyes widened my understanding of the word and of her potential.

Jesus, in his earthly life, sought out the ordinary and elevated it to the extra-ordinary by his deep appreciation and valuing and loving of it.

He saw through to the centre of people with new eyes and turned them inside out.

Figs grew upon thorns; perceptions were changed; self-respect bloomed where formerly there was none; cowards became brave; lepers were embraced and became healthy and whole.

Like my small son with the insect, he gave them a new identity: no longer 'it', but 'she' or 'he'.

Surely, to find beauty in unexpected places, to be able to look at the world with clear-eyed childlike wonder, to appreciate and to value and to love the deeply unlovable, must be one of the great secrets of heaven; one of God's greatest gifts.

Is it, I wonder, given to all children – only to be lost by the majority of us as we grow into adulthood?

And yet, as Jesus so often taught, if you want something badly enough and pray for it and believe you have it – that is, act as if you have it – it will be yours. Presumably that must apply to clear-eyed childlike wonder, too.

Perhaps though, it is easier on the whole for most of us not to want it, for what new things might be expected of us if we began to see beauty where formerly we saw none?

Can you imagine how it would be?

Implacable enemies, from individual ones through to national ones, would begin to appreciate the other in all their wonderful diversity; great companies that pollute the environment would start to re-evaluate their priorities and policies; governments, whose pursuit of wealth and power had been their main – maybe their only – focus, would begin to see the rights of the poor, the vulnerable and the dispossessed in a new light.

Society, the whole human race, would be revolutionised if we all began to recognise the implicit beauty and potential and value in all things and all people.

A whole chain of events would be set in motion. Who knows where it would end? Maybe even with the Kingdom of Heaven being built here on Earth.

And all because we began to see the world through God's eyes.

On the card I use as a marker in my diary is the picture of a glorious sunrise.
The water and the mountains are stained with the myriad heavenly colours of the sky. There is a fresh new glow and promise in it all, that catches and holds me each time I look at it.
At the top are the words,

'Keep Looking Up'.

It reminds me daily that eyes cast down to where my feet are rushing cannot, at the same time, be directed towards the source of all that is beautiful.

I lift up my eyes to the mountains . . .
(Psalm 121:1)

It is a beautiful time,
calm and peaceful and free,
a holy hour,
time-suspended and breathless
with silent adoration.

One of the most beautiful people I have ever met
was a young woman
in a back and neck brace, and in daily constant pain,
but whose face glowed with a shy sweetness
and tenderness and joy.

The apparently mundane and the plain,
Jesus,
that was your speciality.
With the clear-eyed
perception of a child
– or a God –
you knelt in the dust of
life beside them,
gathered them up and
elevated them to a new
understanding of their worth.
You
turned people inside out,
seeing the inner beauty
– the beauty-potential-factor –
thereby transforming
the outer as well.

It is a beautiful time,
calm and peaceful and free,
a holy hour,
time-suspended and breathless
with silent adoration
of you in all
you have made.
Widen my understanding,
extend my vision,
enlarge my heart
to know beauty where
formerly I experienced none,
not just in a holy hour
but at all times,
in all places
and in every one.

Amen.

Frightened

Perfect love casts out fear.
(1 John 4:18)

'Yes, yes – that's all very well. But what does it *mean?*' Marie asked, the frustration plain in her tone. She waved the paper someone had given her, on which the text was written, at me.

Life had been dealing her a lot of bad cards in a short period of time, and now she felt near the edge of the limits of her endurance.

She was a practical person and at first she had faced each difficult event square on, finding ways to use her natural energy and optimism to help her through. She had also, with true Polyanna zeal, looked for the positive within the negative and focused on that.

However, gradually, her energy and her creative attitude had been worn down, and now she felt weary and drained.

'I am just so frightened', she said. 'Every morning I wake up with my stomach knotted up, and feeling sick. I am frightened to go out, and frightened to stay in. My whole life seems now to be ruled by fear.

'The doctor has been good and understanding, and has given me some pills, but I don't feel they are the real solution although they have helped a lot. I don't want to be on pills. I want to find another way of dealing with all of this so that next time I have a bad run – if there *is* a next time, heaven forbid! – I shan't end up feeling the way I do now.

'I am a coper, and it hasn't done my self-image any good at all to end up feeling in a mess inside.'

Marie was, as usual, being hard on herself. As a perfectionist she was never satisfied with what she did, whatever it was. She had, I thought, shown a lot of courage and tenacity in dealing with everything.

Fear is a natural part of our human make-up, and has always been essential for our human survival when, especially as in our early history, there have been plenty of dangerous and threatening things to be fearful of. It is all part of the process which puts our bodies on a kind of red alert, and gets us ready for 'fight or flight'.

However, a lot of situations require both the courage and steadfastness of fight, or staying, as well as inducing in us a deep desire to get as far as possible away from it, or flight – just like Marie's mixture of feelings.

Fear comes in everyday life when we feel out of control of things; when whatever we do seems to have little or no effect on the inexorable grinding onward of a particular course of events. It's a bit like being in the path of a steamroller with little or no chance of being able to get out of the way before it flattens you.

However, when we shift the locus of final control from ourselves to another point, then we begin to realise when we are asking too much of ourselves. There are always some things in life we just cannot control, however much we would like to, and we run through our precious and finite energy by trying to.

True wisdom lies, it seems to me, in knowing when to expend energy in changing a situation, and when to draw in your energy in order to direct it to the task of accepting and, maybe, enduring.

> 'Lord,
> give me the courage to change the things I can change,
> the patience to live with the things I cannot change,
> and the wisdom to know the difference',

so prayed Reinhold Niebhur.

Jesus' life taught us just that – that there are active times and passive times: times when you are able to work to change things, as when he walked the Holy Land preaching and teaching, healing and raising; and times when you must accept, as he did during Holy Week.

By handing over the control to God at the beginning of his ministry, and by continuing to hand it over on a day-by-day basis, he knew when to struggle against situations, and when to put up with them.

'But *how* does perfect love cast out fear?' Marie had asked.

Well, there does not seem to be some magical instant-result formula but rather, like most worthwhile things, it needs to be worked at.

It is not easy to hand over the controls to someone else, especially when that someone else is unseen. It takes faith. It takes belief.

The way I see it is that the perfect love is God's. The fear is ours. When we put the two together there is a synthesis.

When we ask for – and allow – God's love to flow over us, to seep into every part, to slip even between 'joint and marrow', then a mysterious thing begins to happen. A mysterious peace begins to pervade. We begin to realise that, although the process of handing over the control was scary in itself, now we are going in God's strength and not ours.

'My power is at full stretch in your weakness',

God told St Paul (2 Corinthians 12:9), when he prayed that a particularly troublesome burden be taken from him which was, so Paul thought, limiting his activities.

The more desperate we are, the more bowed down, the greater is God's ability to work in us, for then we are less resistant to his love and his strength.

Fear in all its shapes and forms is such a common human condition and so, as is the way in the Scriptures, there are many references to it.

> I sought the Lord and he answered me;
> he delivered me from all my fears.
> (Psalm 34:4)

> God is our refuge and strength,
> an ever present help in trouble,
> therefore we will not fear . . .
> (Psalm 46:1f)

> There is no fear in love.
> But perfect love drives out fear,
> because fear has to do with punishment [consequences].
> (1 John 4:18)

These are just a few examples. There are many, many more.

Jesus was always saying 'Do not be afraid', to those whom he met. He, of all people, must have seen again and again how fear was at the root of so much else, and that he had to exorcise, or get rid of, fear first before he could accomplish anything else in that person's life.

> Lord,
> I'm frightened!
> *So* frightened.
> It's pressing in on me
> like that medieval torture
> cell where the walls
> closed in.
>
> I've tried so hard,
> Lord,
> to overcome it, but
> the more I struggle the
> worse it gets.

'Pull yourself together!'
I scold myself,
yet the unravelling
continues.

Enter in to this
fragmenting fear,
this nightmare.

Bind me together with
your Love.

Amen.

Do not be afraid,
for I am with you;
do not be alarmed,
for I am your God.
I give you strength,
truly I help you,
truly I hold you firm
with my saving right hand.
(Isaiah 41:10)

Thankfulness

> Always be joyful;
> pray constantly;
> and for all things give thanks;
> this is the will of God for you in Christ Jesus.
> (1 Thessalonians 5:16-18)

'Isn't it a bit hypocritical to give thanks for things you are extremely *un*-thankful for?' asked Tom. 'I can't bear that sort of sugary religion that doesn't allow the expression of your real feelings: the fixed-grin crowd I call them.'

We were in a discussion group, and the theme for that day was 'Thankfulness'.

'Yes', said someone else. 'I know exactly what you mean. I was *so* cross – and upset – when someone told me it was a lack of faith to be sad about my husband's death. I didn't go back to that church after that.'

'No, no. You've got it all wrong', said a third. 'It's about giving thanks *in spite of* all the bad things, the sad things, that are happening to you; kind of looking for the silver-lining-round-the-dark-cloud sort of thing. There's good to be found in most situations, however bad.'

'What's good about my husband dying?' retorted the second speaker heatedly.

As the discussion continued, I was reminded of the following:

> There is a Chinese story of an old farmer who had an old horse for tilling his fields. One day the horse escaped into the hills and when all the farmer's neighbours sympathised with the old man over his bad luck, the farmer replied, 'Bad luck? Good luck? Who knows?'
>
> A week later the horse returned with a herd of wild

horses from the hills and this time the neighbours congratulated the farmer on his good luck. His reply was, 'Good luck? Bad luck? Who knows?'

Then, when the farmer's son was attempting to tame one of the wild horses, he fell off its back and broke his leg. Everyone thought this was very bad luck. Not the farmer, whose only reaction was, 'Bad luck? Good luck? Who knows?'

Some weeks later the army marched into the village and conscripted every able-bodied youth they found there. When they saw the farmer's son with his broken leg they let him off.

Now was that good luck? Bad luck? Who knows?

Everything that seems on the surface to be an evil may be a good in disguise. And everything that seems good on the surface may really be an evil. So we are wise when we leave it to God to decide what is good luck and what bad, and thank him that all things turn out for good with those who love him. (43)

I shared the story with the group, then added, 'I wonder then, do you think that to give thanks for all things is in fact to love God with your whole heart? Not in the "fixed-grin" way of Tom's description, but by endeavouring to live as completely in the present moment as possible, engaging with it as fully as possible, and so realising its potential, and your own potential, within that moment and that setting.

'The past has gone, and the future has yet to come. Now, this present moment, is our greatest reality.'

'Yes,' said someone who had not spoken up till then, 'Jesus told us, didn't he, "Do not be anxious for tomorrow, for tomorrow has enough troubles of its own." I don't think he was being pessimistic; rather telling us that if we spend a disproportionate amount of time dreaming and planning for the future, we will not have the proper amount of energy to live today to the full: that tomorrow will as likely not be as we anticipated or feared; so what is the point?'

'I guess,' added Tom, 'to love God with your whole heart *is* to say a wholehearted Yes to life and all that life brings with it. How does it go . . .?

> "For all that has been, Thanks.
> To all that shall be, Yes." (44)

'I just think that's so clever. And I think to be open to life *now*, and to say "Thanks" and "Yes", is to put the past and the future where they belong – in God's hands.'

At the end of our group discussion, we agreed to Tom's suggestion that we spend the last few moments writing down all the things for which we needed to be grateful.

Two unexpected things happened:

The first was that we had to extend the meeting as we were so busily scribbling away. The more we wrote, the more we could think of to write. It was as if a great Aladdin's Cave had opened up, full of half-forgotten treasures. Eventually, we had reluctantly to put our uncompleted lists on one side to be continued at the next meeting, which we decided to devote to our lists, and then to sharing them with each other.

The other strange thing – or maybe it wasn't strange at all – was that in the very act of remembering we began to change. The task, somewhat dutifully and self-consciously started, began to catch us up and so was transformed. We shared how our hearts and minds and eyes had filled up with thankfulness for all these blessings that God had poured and continued to pour down on us. Page after page was filled with enthusiastic scribbles, as the greatest and the smallest blessings were recalled and recorded.

'Thank you.'

'Thank you for the present.'
'Thank you for having me.' . . .
From our earliest childhood
we learn to chant these
words dutifully at times when maybe we do
not mean 'thank you' at all.

So now,
Lord,
now that I want to say
thank you
with all my heart
to you,
how sadly inadequate, how
pale and bland
these words seem –
battered and bruised
and tatty round the edges, too,
from insincere over-usage.

Perhaps, though,
when I learn to move from
head to heart and
allow the words to be
lit up from inside me, I
recreate the world of
meaning, the tender gentle
gratitude of a Jesus:

'Thank you, Martha,
for so lovingly preparing my food.'
'Thank you, Mary,
for listening.'
'Thank you, Peter and John,
for being my friends.'

'Thank you, gentle one, for the oil so tenderly
poured as libation over my feet and head.'
'Thank you for not deserting me
at my hour of need.'
'Most of all,
thank you,
Father,
for the opportunity and the privilege
to give my life
for my friends.'

Now the words are re-created
and recharged with richest meaning,
made holy once more,
blessed
and
transformed.

THANK YOU,
LORD,

THANK YOU!

Amen.

He did not say,

'You shall not be tempest-tossed,

you shall not be work-weary,

you shall not be discomforted';

But he said,

'You shall not be overcome'.

God wants us to heed these words

so that we shall always be strong in

trust,

both in

sorrow

and in

joy.

MOTHER JULIAN OF NORWICH

... It is right

it should be so;

We are made for

Joy

and

Woe;

And when this

we rightly know,

On through life

we safely go.

WILLIAM BLAKE
from Auguries of Innocence

REFERENCES

No.	Page	
1	18	Thomas Merton.
2	19	Gerard Manley Hopkins: *The Habit of Perfection*, OUP. 1986.
3	21	Anthony de Mello SJ: *One Minute Wisdom*, Gujarat Sahitya Prakash, Anand, India. 1987.
4	22	Walter de la Mare: *The Listener*
5	22	Bishop Phillips Brooks: 'O Little Town of Bethlehem'. *Hymns Old & New*.
6	24	Marcus Tullius Cicero (106-43 BC): *De Officius*, III.i.I.
7	29	A Christian Doctor: source not known.
8	29	Albert Einstein: source not known.
9	30	Fynn: *Mister God this is Anna*. William Collins, Sons and Co., Ltd. 1974.
10	31	Anthony de Mello SJ: *Sadhana: A Way to God*, Gujarat Sahitya Prakash, Anand, India.
11	34	Tolstoy: source not known.
12	34	Elyse Bartlett: 4-year-old, who was the first to undergo a hole-in-the-heart treatment that avoids surgery, in May 1996.
13	36	William Shakespeare.
14	39	Immanuel Kant: *Critique of Practical Reason*, Conclusion.
15	40	Anthony de Mello SJ: *One Minute Wisdom*, Gujarat Sahitya Prakash, Anand, India. 1987.
16	41	Alexander Solzhenitsyn: source not known.
17	51	Richard Lovelace: *To Althea, from prison*, in *London Book of English Verse*. Selected by Herbert Read and Bonamy Dobree. Eyre and Spottiswoode. 1949.
18	51	William L. Wallace.
19	55	G. Matheson: *Hymns Old & New*. 1986.
20	56	Caroline Norton: *Not Lost but Gone Before*.
21	58	Anon: *A Crabbit Old Woman*.
22	61	Cardinal Henry Newman: *The Dream of Gerontius*.

23	62	Alfred Lord Tennyson: *Ulysses* I.6.
24	67	Horace: 65-8 BC.
25	69	Taken from GMB General Union list of 50 'reasons' given by employers for cutting jobs.
26	71	Horace. Ibid.
27	72	Alan Ecclestone: In conversation with the author, Holy Week, 1984, The Queen's College, Birmingham.
28	73	Alan Ecclestone: Ibid.
29	81	Victor Frankl: *The Doctor and the Soul.* Vintage Books. 1986.
30	81	Victor Frankl: Ibid.
31	83	Hildegard of Bingen: 1098-1179.
32	85	Joseph Mohr: 'Silent Night'. *Hymns Old & New.*
33	88	William Shakespeare: *Macbeth*, V.iii.40.
34	89	Alfred Lord Tennyson: *The Princess.*
35	94	Lewis Carroll: *Alice in Wonderland.*
36	96	Thomas Hardy: *Far from the Madding Crowd.*
37	99	Lauren Mead: source not known.
38	103	Attributed to Toki Miyashina in *The Lion Book of Famous Prayers,* Lion, 1983, and found in *Still Waters, Deep Waters,* edited by Rowland Crowther, Albatross Books, 1987.
39	108	Heine, found in *The Bible in Art – The Old Testament,* Phaidon Publishers Inc. 1956.
40	121	William Shakespeare: *King Henry VI, Part 2,* III.ii.
41	123	Anthony de Mello SJ: *The Elder Son* (slightly adapted), *The Song of the Bird,* Gujarat Sahitya Prakash, Anand, India. 1983.
42	127	John Keats: *Endymion,* Bk. I.1.1.
43	137	Anthony de Mello SJ: *Sadhana: A Way to God,* Gujarat Sahitya Prakash, Anand, India.
44	138	Dag Hammarskjöld: former UN Secretary General.

All other meditations, poems, etc., if unacknowledged, are the work of the author. Anecdotes as on page 121, if unacknowledged, are stories in general circulation with no known source.